Words by the Way

Words by the Way

Ideas and resources for use throughout
the Christian year

Ann Lewin

British Library Cataloguing in Publication data

A catalogue record for this book is available
from the British Library

ISBN 1-85852-278-1

978-1-85852-278-4

First published by Inspire
4 John Wesley Road
Werrington
Peterborough PE4 6ZP

Printed and bound in Great Britain by
Athenaeum Press Ltd, Gateshead, Tyne & Wear

Dedication

This book is dedicated to Ron, Nigel and Gary, whose friendship and prayerful support over the years have been a great source of encouragement.

There are also many other individuals and groups who, by inviting me to lead events or address a variety of audiences, have given me opportunities to explore fresh ways of communicating the gospel. I have received many blessings from these companions on the way, and I am immensely grateful to them for their challenge and their insights.

Thanksgiving

Given so much,
What have I done to
Deserve it?
Nothing,
Absolutely nothing.
No wonder my heart
Dances.

Ann Lewin

Foreword

It is important for Christians to make connections between our experience of church worship and our ongoing prayer and spiritual life. *Words by the Way* gives us a good opportunity to do this. Taking us through the cycle of the Church's year, Ann Lewin offers us both a resource for personal reflection (with encouragement about how we might approach our everyday praying) and an imaginative range of liturgical material that picks up the themes and imagery of each season in turn.

The shape of the Church's year reminds us of the great drama of our creation and salvation, and every time and season contains an invitation to place our own story, and that of our world, within the unfolding story found in Scripture. Yet we can sometimes be so busy or preoccupied that the richness and flavour of the different parts of the Christian year simply pass us by, and we miss the spiritual treasures within the fabric of each particular season. Ann's book may help us to recover some of these things, such as the wonderful sense of anticipation in Advent, the beauty and mystery of Epiphany, the prayerful possibilities of Good Friday, and the significance of lesser known festivals such as Lammastide.

In her introduction Ann says that she hopes her material 'will spark off creativity in people looking for fresh ways to present truths about God and ourselves'. I can envisage several ways in which this could happen. Some readers who feel that their prayer life is in a rut may find that this book opens up new ways of relating to God through the year. The practical suggestions on pages 18-19 would be a good place to start for those who are not sure where to go next in their prayer life. In addition, I am sure that people responsible for leading worship, or events such as Quiet Days, will welcome the liturgical material and suggestions. This book might also inspire a group within a congregation to organize a special event for carers (pp. 173ff), the setting up of a Quiet Garden (pp. 176ff), or a day exploring the teaching of someone like Julian of Norwich (pp. 166ff). Ann's ideas may also encourage readers to take other creative initiatives of their own, using the sort of outlines and practical suggestions that she gives.

This book is earthed in the realities of daily life, and its journey through the seasons frequently connects us with ordinary experiences. At the same time, there are many glimpses of heaven, for example in the section for Easter Eve:

> Lord Christ, set us on fire,
> burn from us all that dims your light;
> kindle an answering flame in lives around,
> that darkness may be driven back,
> and glory stream into this world,
> transforming it with light. (p. 115)

Ann has the knack of offering us lots of ideas without trying to control or dictate what we do. That is probably because of her own deep understanding of what prayer is about:

> Prayer is like watching for the
> Kingfisher. All you can do is
> Be where he is likely to appear and
> Wait. (p. 27)

Prayer and worship are about waiting on God with open and generous hearts, rather than trying to control God or make things happen to suit ourselves. One way in which we can grow in this openness to God is when our corporate worship and our personal prayer flow into each other and nourish each other. By using this book we may find that dream becoming more of a reality.

Angela Ashwin
Writer and lecturer on spirituality

Acknowledgements

I am grateful to many people who have contributed to the production of this book.

Gary Philbrick read the text in preparation, and made many helpful suggestions from a potential user's point of view. In addition, he has come to my rescue on several occasions when my computer has tried to get the upper hand.

The editorial staff at Inspire have been unfailingly helpful, especially Lorna Lackenby, who has produced another splendid cover, and Natalie Watson and Susan Hibbins who have kept a watchful eye on the text. I take full responsibility for the contents.

Contents

Contents

Introduction

This book is a collection of material I have devised and used over several years. It contains reflections on the significance of seasons and festivals, as well as schemes for use in Workshops, Quiet Days, Retreats and Courses. There are suggestions for liturgy also, including some Eucharistic Prayers, and a simple order for the Eucharist in which these prayers can be used. The prayers were originally written for specific groups, but they have been adapted for other use also. My aim is always to use as few words as possible to say what needs to be said, and to leave space for people to respond to God as God moves them.

The first two sections of the book reflect the events of Jesus' life as the Church's year unfolds. The third section is more diverse, offering responses to the opportunities daily life affords to meet God.

Much of what I offer draws on my own poetry, published in 2004 by Inspire in *Watching for the Kingfisher*, a collection combining some new work with poems previously published in *Candles and Kingfishers* and *Flashes of Brightness*.

I hope that what I offer here will spark off creativity in people looking for fresh ways to present truths about God and ourselves as we explore the riches of God's love anew, year by year.

Ann Lewin
May 2005

Section 1

Advent to Candlemas

Advent

There's little doubt about what most of us will be doing in the next four weeks – the Christmas rush to get everything organized, cards written, gifts bought and sent, the preparation of food, plans about whose turn it is to go visiting, and anxieties about who'll be offended if we don't pay them enough attention .... The rush is on, and it's not surprising that there's often a hint of panic in people's conversations – 'I'll never be ready!'

In four weeks it'll all be over, in five a new year will have brought us another set of resolutions, in six the decorations will have come down, the furniture of life will be back in place, and we'll be back to – what? Will life be just the same, or will we be changed? If we take Advent seriously, I hope we *will* be changed, because we shall have had the opportunity to reflect again on what it means to say that God came into the world in the humility of the birth at Bethlehem, and that he still comes into the world in all its mess and pain and joy, longing for us to recognize him.

Advent is a godsend, a gift which stops us in our tracks, and makes us realize that we hold dual citizenship (of this world and the kingdom) in awkward tension. We are part of the scene – Christians sometimes appear to be rather superior about what we call commercialization, and say that the real Christmas isn't about that. But the real Christmas is about precisely that: it's about God coming into the real world, not to a sanitised stable as we portray it in carols and on Christmas cards, but to a world that needed, and still needs, mucking out. Advent reminds us that the kingdom has other themes to add to the celebration, themes that are there in the Scripture readings for the season: Repent, be ready, keep awake, he comes.

Advent reminds us that not only do we live in two worlds, the one that appears to be going mad all around us, and the one that lives by the kingdom of God's values, but that we operate in two different time scales, in chronological time, and beyond it. And the point of intersection is *now*. Passages of Scripture read during Advent, and the *Prayer Book* collect for Advent which is often used, remind us that *now* is the time when we have to cast away the works of darkness, and put on the armour of light. *Now* is when we meet God, because we have no other time.

At whatever level we operate, it's a time for preparation. And whatever else we have to do, there are only so many *praying* days to Christmas. It is prayer that gives us the opportunity to focus our recognition of God in every part of our lives. Prayer is not just what we do in what we call our prayer time. Prayer is how we give our relationship with God a chance to grow and develop and, just like any other relationship, it needs time. We don't stop being related when we are not with the person concerned. We don't stop being a wife, husband, child, parent or friend when that person is out of sight, or when we are concentrating on something else. But we become less of a related person if we never give them time.

So, Advent says, make time, create a space so that our understanding of God's love for us, and our love for God in response can grow. The world is saying, 'Get on with it – don't wait for Christmas to hold the celebrations.' Advent says, 'Wait, be still, alert and expectant.'

Some people find it helpful to have a focal point for their stillness; perhaps a lit candle. Any candle will do, but there are candles with the days marked on them, so that we don't have any excuse for not remembering. And using a candle like this reminds us that before there were clocks people used candles to measure time. Christmas is bound up with time as well as eternity. We're celebrating God becoming involved in our world in Jesus, and God invites us to make time for him.

The shopping days will come to an end – there will come a moment when we really can't do any more. But the point of the praying days is that we get into the habit of remembering God who comes to us every day, and longs for us to respond with our love and service.

Eucharistic Prayer for Advent

Lord God, you come to us
in the simplicity of a baby,
yet are greater by far than our imagining:
Come to us, Lord.

Lord Christ, you hide your ways from
the proud,
yet reveal your truth to those of a
childlike spirit:
Come to us, Lord.

Lord Spirit, you overthrow the powerful,
yet empower the humble and open of heart:
Come to us, Lord.

Come to us now in your vulnerable strength,
as we remember Jesus,
who brought wholeness and life
through his death and resurrection.
On the night before he died,
he took bread and wine, blessed them
and gave them to his friends, saying,
'This is my body, this is my blood.
Eat and drink to remember me.'

Come freshly to us, living God;
bring in your kingdom of justice and love:
Your kingdom come.

Heal us, that we may be whole in your service:
Your kingdom come.

Teach us, that we may be surprised into truth:
Your kingdom come.

For you are the God who longs to set us free
to love and serve you wholeheartedly:
**Your kingdom come in us, Lord,
and transform the world
to your praise and glory. Amen.**

Eucharistic Prayer – The kingdom

Lord God,
your kingdom is here and not yet,
hidden, yet ours for the seeking:
Your kingdom come.

Your kingdom requires of us total commitment,
and gives us unlimited freedom:
Your kingdom come.

Your kingdom turns our values upside down,
for your King rules through suffering love:
Your kingdom come.

With angels and archangels,
and all whose lives
have been changed by your kingdom,
we praise you, saying:
Holy, holy, holy Lord,
king of joy and love,
heaven and earth are full of your glory,
all praise to your name.

Come to us now, most loving God,
as we remember Jesus, who
on the night before he died,
took bread and wine, blessed them,
and gave them to his friends, saying,
'This is my body, this is my blood.
Eat and drink, all of you.'

Come freshly to us now, Lord God.
Open our eyes to the signs of your kingdom:
Your kingdom come.

Call us again to commit ourselves to your service:
Your kingdom come.

Send your Holy Spirit,
that your life and vitality may flow through us,
and change the lives of all we meet:
Your kingdom come in us, Lord,
and transform the world,
to your praise and glory. Amen.

Thinking about prayer

'Have you done your practice? Have you said your prayers?'

Those are two questions I remember from my childhood. Odd questions ... no one in the house could have failed to notice whether I had done my practice. And my mother was always in the house. The other question seemed a bit intrusive. Whether I'd said my prayers or not seemed to be my affair, not anyone else's. But my discomfort at being asked the question arose more from the fact that on the occasion I remember, I had to say 'no'. And I got the distinct impression that that was the wrong answer!

Reflecting later, I realized that these were not really questions at all, but a bit of parental control, making sure that I did the important things – rather like 'Have you cleaned your teeth?' And further reflection, much later on, made me think that *as* questions, they entirely missed the point. Doing my practice, saying my prayers were not activities for their own sake, to be done, ticked off for the day and then forgotten about until the next parental nudge; they both led on to something greater. Piano practice was important because it was part of becoming more musical – something those within earshot must have hoped would happen sooner, rather than later. And saying my prayers was part of growing more prayerful, part of establishing that relationship with God which is the foundation of all Christian living. I wonder if it would have been more helpful if I had been asked 'Have you become more musical today? Have you become more prayerful?'

Prayer is an expression of our relationship with God – and one of the other things about it that I eventually realized is that *saying* my prayers, like practising scales, was only the beginning: my practice needed to spill over into the whole of my life. Because that is what relationships are like. We don't stop being related when we are not consciously present with the person with whom we are in relationship. The relationship continues as we go about the ordinary things of life. We may think of the person we relate to from time to time – 'John would be interested in this; I must remember to tell Mary'.... And from time to time, regularly, we need time with the other person to catch up, get to know them better, enjoy their company. I know that I don't play the piano nearly as well now that I don't practise. We all know of relationships that drift or founder because we don't make time for them.

So our prayer time is the time when we practise the presence of God, so that *all* our life may be filled with the presence of God. Most people think that behaviour matters and prayer helps it. The truth is that prayer matters, and behaviour tests it.[1]

One of the odd things about our Christian life is that on the whole we don't talk about prayer. I had piano lessons which didn't just test how I was getting on, but gave me and the teacher a chance to look at techniques that would help – a difficult passage would become easier to cope with if I sorted the fingering out, or a piece of music might come to life if I played some of it more quietly, and didn't just hit the notes .... But I didn't have much help with learning to pray. It was something that on the whole I was left to get on with. We went to church, there was the odd sermon, but I don't remember anyone saying to me, 'How are you getting on with your prayer life?' So I suppose I grew up thinking that I was supposed to know about prayer, and that everyone else already knew. That is what we do think, probably. We look around and see everyone else devoutly concentrating, and don't realize that behind the closed eyes and clasped hands, there is as much confusion and inattention as there is in us.

There is a skit by Joyce Grenfell in which she is shown in church singing a hymn: 'Calm and untroubled are my thoughts' – and then we realize that she is singing what she is actually thinking about – she forgot to turn the gas down under the saucepan of chicken bones she was turning into stock; she imagines the pan boiling dry, the stove, then the house, catching fire; where will they sleep tonight? If she goes home now, she might be in time to save the picture which is supposed to be a Picasso, though she'd much rather save her photograph album .... She turns to her husband and sings, 'I suppose you didn't think to check the gas? No, I didn't think you would have.' The skit ends with her singing again, 'Calm and untroubled are my thoughts'.

It's funny not just because it's Joyce Grenfell, but because it rings true for us all. We all find it difficult to concentrate, to find time – we get stuck in ways of praying that perhaps we need to grow on from. We have to learn to move from having a time of prayer to having a life of prayer. That takes practice. Unlike the piano practice, there are no exams – we're not going to be better than the people who've only passed Grade III. The aim is not to be 'good' at prayer – I don't know what that would mean – but to be faithful in establishing the prayerfulness of the whole of life. There is nothing that can't be prayerful. If we can think of anything that can't be prayerful, perhaps we need to question whether we should be doing it at all.

Nothing that can't be prayerful. There's the story of two monks who argued about whether you could drink coffee and pray at the same time. They couldn't agree, so they went off to ask their spiritual directors for advice. When they came back, they still couldn't agree. One monk said, 'My director said, "No, on no account must you let anything interfere with prayer."' The other monk said, 'That's odd, my director didn't think there was a problem at all. What did you ask?'

The first monk said, 'I asked if I could drink coffee while I was praying, and my director got quite cross with me.'

The other laughed. 'Oh, I asked whether I could pray while I was drinking coffee.'

It's all about changing our attitudes, about growing into a deeper understanding. What we are about is coming closer to the God who loves us – and our response to that love can be expressed in the words of Julian of Norwich, that wise woman from the fourteenth century. She prayed, 'God, of your goodness give us yourself; for if we ask anything that is less, we shall always be in want. Only in you we have all.'[2]

Notes

1. After William Temple, 'The proper relation in thought between prayer and conduct is not that conduct is supremely important and prayer may help it, but that prayer is supremely important, and conduct tests it.' From *Christus Veritas*, published Macmillan, London 1924. Quoted by Gordon Mursell in *English Spirituality: From 1700 to the Present Day, vol. 2, p. 373*, SPCK.

2. *Revelation of Divine Love*, Long Text ch. 5.

Material for a workshop on ways of praying

The material on pp. 18-19 has been used in many different ways: as the basis for a day, an evening, a Lent course, and for a retreat. The intention is to broaden people's understanding of prayer, to give them space to explore different ways of praying, and to have the opportunity to talk about their own prayer life, its joys and difficulties, in a way that we don't often have the chance to do.

No one comes to this subject as an expert, but we all have experience, and it is helpful to share it – if only because it is such a relief to find that other people's experience is often uncannily like our own.

It is helpful to begin by asking people to talk to their neighbour for a few minutes, identifying what they hope to get out of the event. After that, it is easier to have a general discussion in the group, and list any points people want to raise.

Often, an inability to concentrate is high on the list. It is worth dealing with that problem early in the proceedings. We don't concentrate on anything for very long – mostly we have a lot of things on our minds, and we juggle with them to prioritize. We don't suddenly change when we decide to spend time in prayer! But we also know that sometimes we get caught up in something, and don't know where the time has gone. Setting aside time for prayer means that we put ourselves where God can catch our attention, and then we can leave the prayer to God. For prayer is always a gift, it is God who prays in us and transforms us, rather than we who achieve great heights of devotion. We don't have to beat ourselves up about the fact that we are creatures with a short attention span – when we find our thoughts wandering off, we can gently bring ourselves back to God. And the more we practise doing that, the more natural it becomes to find ourselves aware of God's presence.

How much time we can give to consideration of the various ways of praying depends on the nature of the event, but it is always important to give people time to explore for themselves, and have a time for comments and questions. We don't have to do everything on one occasion – an introduction to what is possible may lead fruitfully to follow-up sessions.

The ways of praying illustrated are arranged on the sheet so that those around the edges are methods which require some time to be set aside. Between them are the ideas we can put into practice as we go about daily life. The candle stands for Christ at the centre, and reminds us that prayer is the expression of our relationship with God as we have been shown him in Jesus, and in God we have all. Much has already been written about the ways of praying illustrated, but ideas about exploring some of them further follow the illustration.

Find a way that works for you

Light a candle

Reflect that Jesus is the light of the world.

Remember your baptism – you have been called from the darkness to live in the light.

Celebrate!

Light a prayer for someone – others will draw strength from your light.

Write a Psalm

Look at a Psalm (Psalm 77 perhaps). Notice its absolute honesty about feelings, and what it says about God. Try writing your own.

Spend time with an icon

Let it speak to you, draw you into its inner meaning.

Go for a walk

Look at what is around you. Give thanks for what is good. Look at the Benedicite (in Anglican Morning Prayer service) Make up your own version: O . . . bless ye the Lord . . . *Touch* – enjoy the texture of tree-trunk, stone, fabric . . . *Listen* – enjoy the peace, or use the sounds you hear as material for prayer: police siren or birdsong can each start you off.

Read the paper

Don't get sucked in – set statements of faith against reported news, (the psalms will give you ideas). Put your arm around those who make the news, and hold them before God.

Sing and make melody to the Lord. Laments and protests too.

Adoration
Confession
Thanksgiving
Supplication

} These **ACTS**
are a good
basis for prayer

Draw or paint

Go on a pilgrimage

Pilgrimage is about visiting places and recognizing that God has been at work there. You can go to holy places: you can also recognize the holiness of ordinary places. Try looking at the street you live in, the rooms of your home, different parts of your body. Remember God is concerned about each of them – make the connections.

Carry a prayer around

Use it when your mind is in neutral – at the supermarket checkout, in a traffic jam – much more constructive than cursing delay! The Jesus prayer* or Taizé chants are good.

*Lord Jesus Christ,
Son of God, have mercy.*

Spend time

thinking about what you have read in the Bible or another book which points you to God.

Use an 'office' –

morning or evening prayer. Make up a basic kit for yourself – Psalm, reading, prayers.

Practise stillness

Let God have a chance.

Don't try to think – gently repeat a short prayer, let it focus your mind, take you deep.

Dance!
If your
joints will
let you.

Let go and let God

Using the Psalms

The Psalms are a very rich resource, tested and tried in many situations. People often have their favourite quotations, which they call to mind as appropriate. As well as providing words of comfort or encouragement, the Psalms show us a way of bringing all our feelings to God. They give us words to use to express our joy and trust; they also give us words to use when we are angry or in despair. They offer us a model of setting alongside the awfulness of life a statement about God, sometimes linked with a *'nevertheless'*. They do not ask us to resolve our problems by saying that everything is going to be all right. They ask us to face the difficulty, and hold it in tension with what we believe about God, and wait.

We are sometimes worried by the intensity of our feelings, and think that we can't let God know how angry and violent we feel. After all, 'nice' people don't think or say the things we would really like to express! But actually there is nothing in the Christian gospel about being 'nice'. There is plenty about being loving and just, and straight in our dealings with others. Sometimes the only right response is anger. There is nothing about us that God does not already know, and nothing about us that will stop God loving us, whatever we feel.

It is important to look at the whole of a Psalm, and not leave out the hard verses. Liturgically we may need to omit some verses: it would probably not be very edifying for someone who had just dropped in to see what our worship was like, to hear everyone saying, 'Break their teeth, O God!' (Psalm 58.4). For personal use, though, we need to see the Psalms as they are, and experience the liberation of learning that honesty with God can be the beginning of a vigorous relationship with him.

It is a useful exercise sometimes to write a psalm for ourselves. There is great value in writing out what we feel, especially in times of anger or bewilderment or despair. The process can help us to see the situation in a more objective way, and often cuts it down to size, preventing our imaginations from running away with us in unhelpful ways.

This is how one person at a workshop responded to the invitation to write a psalm.

He was grieving the death of his daughter from leukaemia, and reflected on Psalm 137, set in the *Book of Common Prayer* for use on the 28th evening of the month.

His reflection centred on the last verse of the Psalm: 'Blessed shall he be that taketh thy children: and throweth them against the stones.'

28th Evening

You took our child, God. You threw her on the rocks of cancer. You tortured her little body with surgery and chemotherapy and radiotherapy, and you tortured us with hope. You did that for eighteen months. And then for a year you mocked us, as her hair grew back and that sharp and musical mind flourished as never before.

And then you struck, and the laughter died in our throats. At least you spared us hope the second time.

Now we could only watch with her, and wait, as the talents which seemed about to burst so joyfully from Hannah withered and died. And we talked together of what would be, knowing that as we did, it was only of what might have been.

You threw her against the stones one last time, and she died on the 28th evening – just ten days before her sixth birthday. And I cannot forgive you for that, God. Hannah has, that I know. For all that she endured at your hands, she still went on loving you. Your abused child. Because she didn't know any better. Thank God I do not have her faith, her incapacity to hate.

What were you doing? I was the one with her. I was the one who held her in my arms for the injections. I was the one who calmed her fears during the nose bleeds.

Who held You?
Who gave you strength?
Who so encompassed you around with love that it flowed out from you to Hannah without despair? She could only love me so trustingly because she knew what a Father's love could be.

By the waters of Babylon I sat down and wept – with you. With you from the first morning to the 28th Evening.
And with you now
And with Hannah now
And she with me though I no longer weep for her.
Though still I shall weep with you whenever you visit the waters of Babylon.

Robin Harger
(used with permission)

Praying with icons

Icons are not just pictures, they are windows into the world beyond. They play an important part in the prayer and worship of Eastern Orthodox Christians. They are stylised, painted according to ancient custom by rules handed down through the generations, and are always the fruit of prayerful attention to God. At first sight they may not be very attractive to western eyes, but paying attention to them may draw us deeper into the mystery they represent.

They are painted (Orthodox Christians would say 'written') using a different scheme of perspective from that to which westerners have become accustomed. In western post-Renaissance painting, the lines of perspective lead the eye to a distant point. In many icons, the perspective is reversed, so that our attention becomes focused in front of the icon, between us and it. Sometimes it seems as though the icon is looking at us, instead of the other way round. There is a sense that we are being engaged by the subject. The icons of Mary with the infant Christ, for example, invite us to contemplate the child – the angle of Mary's head, the position of her hands, and the way she holds the child, all point to him: we are invited to give Christ the central place in our worship. The icon of the Holy Trinity gives the impression that the three persons of the Trinity are all paying attention to each other – look at the angle of their heads – and the gap in the front of the circle invites us to join in the conversation.

There is a sense of stillness in icons. The eyes of the characters portrayed seem to be contemplating some inner truth. Mouths are often small, and eyes large – the key to spiritual growth is watchfulness and attention, rather than talking a lot.

It takes time to appreciate what God may be saying to us through an icon – what we have to do is be still before it, and wait.

There are several books which can help us to understand icons better, among them:

Behold the Beauty of the Lord – Praying with Icons, Henri Nouwen, Ave Maria Press, 1987.

Doors of Perception, John Baggley, Mowbray, 1987.

Festival Icons for the Christian Year, John Baggley, Mowbray, 1987.

Praying with Icons, Jim Forrest, Orbis, 1997.

Using silence

'In quietness and in trust shall be your strength'
(Isaiah 30.15).

'For God alone my soul waits in silence' (Psalm 62.1).

'Come away to a deserted place all by yourselves and
rest a while' (Mark 6.31).

There is much in Scripture about God coming to
people in stillness. Our difficulty is that modern life
tries to keep us constantly on the go, and we are in
the habit of filling our airwaves with noise. We have
to make a conscious effort to get away from life's
muzak and listen. When we do that, we discover
another problem: we don't always want to engage in
stillness because we fear what we may discover about
ourselves. We have to remember that God knows us
in the depths of our being, and loves us as we are:
'You are precious in my sight, and honoured, and I
love you' (Isaiah 43.4). That doesn't mean that we
don't need to change, but that we don't need to wait
until we have before we can enjoy God's company. If
there are areas within ourselves which need to be
dealt with, it may be wise to wait until we can work
with a trusted guide.

Stillness and silence are states we have to learn to
relax into, rather than screwing ourselves up to find
them, and there are various techniques which may
help:

- Find a place where you can be relaxed, yet alert.
  Some people find it helpful to have a particular
  place in house or garden which they regard as
  their prayer place.

- Decide how long you are going to spend in this
  way of prayer.

- Light a candle, play some music, use a relaxation exercise to help mind and body to settle.

- Read a short passage of Scripture, select a thought or phrase from it; or use a sentence from a hymn or a prayer. Repeat the phrase gently, in time with your breathing.

- Let yourself become still; let God hold you in love.

- When thoughts do wander, gently re-establish the phrase (or 'rhythm prayer' as some people call it) and allow yourself to become still again. Don't worry if your thoughts wander off. We are usually not very good at concentrating in the normal course of events, and we don't suddenly change when we decide to pray. Wandering thoughts are not something to feel guilty about.

- At the end of the allotted time, gently bring yourself back to awareness of what is around you. (You may need to set a timer or an alarm, but put it in another room, so that it doesn't jolt you back into ordinariness.) Perhaps play some music again, to help you adjust.

- Say a brief prayer of thanksgiving for the opportunity to be still, and for God's presence with you.

Don't worry if nothing much seems to have happened. Prayer is God's gift to us: what we have to do is open ourselves up to the possibility of receiving the gift, and leave the rest to God.

Disclosure

Prayer is like watching for the
Kingfisher. All you can do is
Be where he is likely to appear and
Wait.
Often, nothing much happens;
There is space, silence and
Expectancy.
No visible sign, only the
Knowledge that he's been there
And may come again.
Seeing or not seeing cease to matter,
You have been prepared,
But sometimes, when you've almost
Stopped expecting it
A flash of brightness
Gives encouragement.

Carrying prayer around

When people talk about prayer, it often sounds like a specialized activity. There are many techniques and methods we can use. But as we grow in prayerfulness, we have to learn to take prayer out of the speciality range into general use, to learn how prayer can be a way of life.

Paul said, 'Pray without ceasing' (1 Thessalonians 5.17). We might feel like responding with, 'You must be joking – I've got far too much to do to be able to indulge in prayer all the time.' And at one level that's true. There are things we have to do which demand all our attention. I'm glad when people do pay attention to what they are doing. I wouldn't thank my dentist, for example, if he did anything other than keep his mind on the job!

There is an old saying in Latin, *laborare est orare* – to work is to pray. Doing what we have to do wholeheartedly is prayer. When our lives are offered to God, every part of our life is part of that offering.

Brother Lawrence was a Carmelite monk in the seventeenth century. He was well known for his holiness and his awareness of the presence of God. He wasn't a scholar or a choir monk, he worked in the kitchen amidst all the demands of a busy monastery. People often think of monasteries as places of calm – those who live in them know that it isn't quite like that. Communities, like families, have their tensions. In his time monasteries were very busy places, a cross between a Travelodge and McDonalds, catering not just for those who lived there, but for visitors and pilgrims too.

Brother Lawrence believed that it was important to relate all his life to God, work and prayer alike. He said that his method was simple: he would go to the times of prayer required by his monastery, then he would do his work, asking God to help him to stay in God's presence, and do his work well. When he finished his work, he would examine himself as to how well he had done it. If well, he thanked God, if not, he asked pardon and, without being discouraged, continued to try to stay aware of God's presence. 'The time of business does not differ with me from the time of prayer, and in the noise and clutter of my kitchen, while several persons are at the same time calling for different things, I possess God in as great tranquillity as if I were on my knees at the Blessed Sacrament.'

That is the challenge for us all, to learn to live our lives aware of God's presence. Easier said than done! Brother Lawrence's way of prayer is sometimes called 'The practice of the presence of God'. If we are wondering how on earth we can do it, it is worth remembering that the word that we hear as a noun 'practice', is also a verb, 'practise'.

We have to establish the habit of remembering that there is a connection between God and ourselves wherever we are: walking around, relaxing with friends, shopping – *now* is the time we meet God. Two simple prayers are enough to carry around with us: 'Thank God', and 'Lord, have mercy'. These are the responses we can make to all the circumstances of our lives, for God is concerned with the painful experiences and the hard questions just as much as with the joys and delights.

And God is concerned with the chores too. We can, for example, transform our wait in the supermarket queue by using our imaginations about the people and the trolleys around us. The old man with a loaf and a tin of dog food: what is life like for him? Lord, have mercy on all who live alone. And thank God for the company of pets. The trolley loaded up with drink – is that a celebration, or an addiction? Which prayer do I use? And the mother with screaming children trying to put things she doesn't want in the trolley – Lord, thank you for family life, and have mercy on parents tried beyond their limits by the demands of small children. The carer taking people with learning disabilities on their weekly shopping trip – Lord, have mercy on all who can't join fully in the life around them, and thank God for all who care for them. This is not done in any judgemental way – looking at my own trolley will soon make me realize that I am in no superior position. Do I really need all that I have picked up, or was I seduced by the latest adverts? And did I go for the fairly traded goods, or the brands I really prefer? Lord, have mercy on me, and give me a thankful heart for all the blessings I enjoy.

Praying for the world

'God saw everything that he had made, and indeed, it was very good' (Genesis 1.31).

I wonder what God makes of it now, when he looks at the world. Perhaps, with tears in his eyes, God says, 'What a mess.' But nothing can stop God loving his world. When we engage in intercession, we are saying to God, 'We love your world too, and we want to help you make a difference.'

We can't pray as though the world is something apart from us – we are part of the problem, as well as being potentially part of the solution. Alan Ecclestone wrote in an article about prayer[1] that everything we do, say or think is either prayer or anti-prayer. Intercession is a way of praying that expresses our intention of putting our energy alongside God's energy. We don't simply hand everything over to God for God to sort out, we offer ourselves to God to be used. Intercession is dangerous prayer, for we are quite likely to be challenged with 'What are you going to do about the situation?' We won't all be called out to the troubled spots, but we may well find ourselves being nudged into supporting those who do go. And one of the ways our intercession can be most fruitful is in asking questions of those with power – political pressure is part of this prayer.

It is important to remember those who perpetrate evil, as well as the victims. We sometimes hesitate to do that, because we think that to pray for someone somehow suggests that we are approving of their actions, or praying for their well-being. The 'evil doers' are also loved by God, and our prayer is an expression of our desire that they will know that love for themselves, and experience a change of heart and action. They are only different from us in the degree to which they give reign to their murderous desires – few of us can say that we have never had a desire to harm someone. 'Lord, have mercy' is a prayer that we all need to pray.

It is sometimes helpful to pray using a visual aid, and a physical action. A map of the world can be used in conjunction with various objects:

- Read the vision of the New Jerusalem, Revelation 22.1-2, and invite people to place a leaf on the map.

- Read Julian of Norwich's vision of the hazelnut, (*Revelation of Divine Love*, Long Text ch. 5) and invite people to place a hazelnut on the map.

- Remind people that Jesus is the light of the world, and invite people to place a lit candle on the map.

- The action can be accompanied by a brief spoken prayer.

- (Reassure participants that this is not a Geography test – God understands what we want to pray for even if we are not very sure where in the world it is.)

When sufficient time has elapsed for all who want to take part to do so, draw together all the prayers, spoken aloud or inwardly, in the words of the litany which follows. The response to the petition 'Come, Lord' can be varied according to the situation. 'Let your healing power be known' is one possibility, or 'Let your love be shown'.

End the time by praying that in everything we are, or do, or say or think we may be signs of God's kingdom, as we say the Lord's Prayer together.

Notes

1. Published in *Firing the Clay*, ed. Jim Cotter, Cairns
Publications, 1999.

A litany for the world

In the places of decision-making
and the places of powerlessness:
Come, Lord.

In the places of wealth
and the places of poverty:
Come, Lord.

Where we are healthy
and where we are sick:
Come, Lord.

In the streets of plenty
and in the dark corners and alleys:
Come, Lord.

In our places of worship
And where there is no faith:
Come, Lord.

In our places of learning
and in the depths of our ignorance:
Come, Lord.

In our homes and our welcomes
and where people couldn't care less:
Come, Lord.

Leading intercessions

Being asked to lead the intercessions in a service can strike terror into people's hearts! A workshop drawing on the ideas set out in the section 'Praying for the World' can offer people a chance to look at what is involved, and develop the basic skills required to encourage everyone present to pray.

As well as discussion about what we think the prayer of intercession is, it is helpful to have material for people to look at – there are many books on the market now which give ideas. And it is useful, too, to let people try out the sound system, or see how their voices work in the building used for worship.

When I run a workshop, I normally prepare intercessions for a particular occasion, usually a couple of Sundays ahead, and explain what led me to include or exclude some items which might have been appropriate. Selection is a very important principle – we can't pray for everything every week. World events and local situations can change in the time between the preparation of the prayers, and the service in which they will be used, so it is important to be able to be flexible.

I have drawn up some guidelines which can be useful as a basis for discussion and practice.

- Set the preparation in the context of your own prayer. Ask for the guidance of the Holy Spirit.

- When preparing the prayers, look at the readings and themes for the day. If possible, ask the preacher what the sermon is likely to be about. Look at parish/diocesan/circuit cycles of prayer.

- Select from all the above, and your local knowledge and awareness of what is happening in the world to decide on the areas you want to pray for.

- Look at some of the available books for ideas. You may discover helpful ways of saying things. You do not have to use whole prayers – the odd sentence is often useful.

- When you begin to write your prayers, remember to address them to God.

- Remember to give thanks, as well as to ask.

- Remember how your sentences begin, and keep them consistent. (If you ask for God's blessing *on* someone or some situation, don't, within the same sentence, say *for*.)

- Keep the prayers brief – let people have time for their own thoughts and prayers.

- On the day, have a pen handy, so that you can put in last-minute requests, or respond to something the preacher has said. But don't re-preach the sermon, or try to improve on it!

- When the time comes, wait for people to settle physically, and leave a space for them to gather their thoughts.

- Speak slowly – feel that your pace is slow. Pray the prayers, rather than just saying them.

- Pause. Let spaces grow between the sentences. Give people time to respond inwardly to what you have said.

- Breathe deeply, hold your head up, and look towards the end of the place in which you are speaking. Pitch your voice low (especially women) – that way the sound carries further. Throw your voice to the end of the room.

- If you want to change the response to the petitions, make sure people know what they have to say. Instead of 'Lord, in your mercy' with the response 'Hear our prayer', you might want to say, 'Lord, hear us' with the response 'Graciously hear us'. So tell the congregation, and give them a chance to try it before you continue with the prayers. It is probably best not to change the response in the middle of the prayers.

Leading prayers is your offering to God. You don't have to worry about whether you are as good as other people – this week it's your turn. You may feel nervous, but breathing deeply as people settle down will help you to settle too. People value variety and freshness, so enjoy taking your turn.

The Bible: story and ourselves

'This year,' said a friend of mine, 'I'm going to read the Bible.'

I was rather surprised, for she had always been very scornful of religious practice. I was interested to know more.

'How are you going to set about it?' I asked.

'I'm going to start at the beginning, and read all the way through. Don't tell me it's the wrong way to do it.'

So I didn't. But I could imagine her progress, and almost predict chapter and verse where her resolution would, almost literally, run into the sand. Genesis starts off promisingly, there are some very good stories in it: the Creation, the Flood, the family sagas of Abraham, Isaac and Jacob, and the beautifully told story of Joseph. And the book of Exodus is almost as exciting as the people are freed from slavery in Egypt and journey through the desert, discovering the generous love and care God has for them. But attention begins to waver as the writer presents instructions for the building of the Tabernacle, the size of the altar, the robes for the priests. And after Exodus comes Leviticus, where you have to be really determined to stick with it as laws and rituals about things we don't usually mention in polite conversation are described in minute detail. There are more exciting stories to come, but Leviticus is probably the point at which anyone who thought the Bible was a book to read through from beginning to end would give up.

The Bible isn't a book, but a collection of books, put together at various points in the history of the people whose story it tells, and edited several times in the process. So one of the first things we need to do is to discover the context of what we are reading. (*The Lion Handbook to the Bible* is quite a good starting point.)

And it is helpful, too, to think about the nature of story. Everybody loves a good story. We probably don't remember being read to as children, but bedtime stories are part of the reassurance that everything is under control, ordered. At this point, if at no other during the day, we have someone's undivided attention; we hear a story in which frightening or evil people or powers are inevitably conquered. Stories are the stage on which our fears and terrors can be encountered, in the safe knowledge that good will win. We never tire of hearing them, and woe betide anyone who tries to skip a page.

Stories aren't just about being reassured, feeling secure in the knowledge that everything is under control. They are much more powerful. We use story to discover the roots of our history and our culture. Families bind themselves together, or sometimes destroy each other, by their stories – listen in on a gathering at a wedding or funeral! We use stories when we meet people, and talk about who they are in terms of where they've come from, and where they hope they're going.

But stories are more important even than that. They are ways of engaging our imagination, helping us to explore things about our own personalities. Fairy stories, folk tales, religious stories, biographies, even fiction (however firm the disclaimer that no living person is portrayed in the story) are all written out of experience; all alike give us a framework, a vocabulary for dealing with ideas that are perhaps too painful to deal with directly.

Stories don't necessarily illustrate, make things easy. They involve us, provoke us into response. They sneak past our defences and catch us off guard. The story of David and Bathsheba, and the way Nathan the prophet brought David to an understanding of what he had done illustrates this well (2 Samuel 11 – 12.14).

Apart from the fact that to have gone to the king and told him off for committing adultery and murder might have resulted in an unpleasant experience for Nathan, it would also have put David on the defensive. Telling David a story was a stroke of genius. David got so involved that he couldn't restrain his anger: 'Who is that man? He must die.' And having made his judgement, he can't evade his own story; he takes responsibility for what he has done.

Stories may take us out of ourselves, give us a break, but they give us back to ourselves with deeper understanding, seeing more clearly where our responsibility lies, which in turn frees us from the guilt which so often prevents us from moving on in our lives. And listening to people's stories reassures us that we are not alone – there may not be an obviously happy ending, but there are companions along the way who are closer to us than perhaps we realized.

The Bible is full of stories, and they all contribute to one big story, the story of God's love affair with his people. 'You are precious in my sight, and honoured, and I love you' (Isaiah 43.4). The Bible is not a book of instructions, but an invitation to listen to God's story, which is our story too. God doesn't tell us what to think, God invites us to discover who we are as we follow the events described in the Old Testament, and respond to the challenge of the prophets who, like Nathan, brought people face to face with the consequences of their choices. And in the New

Testament, we meet the Word of God in a fresh way in Jesus, and think about how we might have responded if we had been there with him. What does it mean to be precious in God's eyes? The story of Jesus tells us that it doesn't mean that we will be spoilt. Although Jesus knew himself to be loved, he was not spared the cross, or the feeling of being totally alone. But he also knew that God is faithful, and that nothing in the end will be able to separate us from God's love.

The story of God's love continues as our personal story unfolds. The challenge for us is to discover where God is in the particular circumstances of our lives, or in the world around us. The Bible can help us not so much by giving us the right answers to our questions, but by helping us to ask the right questions, and nudging us into making appropriate responses. When we read the Bible we need to ask, as happens in at least one church at the end of a reading, 'How is this the word of God for us today?'

Intercessions for a Christmas Midnight Service

Glory to God in the highest, and peace to his people on earth. As we hear the angels' song, we join them in worship, and rejoice that you have come among us, Lord God, to be with us for ever. Help us to witness to that truth in our daily lives.

Lord, in your mercy:
Hear our prayer.

Lord, you came among us as Prince of Peace. We pray for peace, especially tonight in Bethlehem and the rest of the Holy Land. We pray that people of all races and creeds throughout the world will learn to live together, respecting each other, and seeking the good of all.

Lord, in your mercy:
Hear our prayer.

Lord God, you came among us as a sign of hope. We pray for all who find hope difficult to hold onto ... refugees, asylum seekers, political prisoners, the hungry and homeless and the unloved. We thank you for those who work to make life better for others, and we pray that we will take every opportunity to help.

Lord, in your mercy:
Hear our prayer.

Lord, you came among us as light. We pray for wisdom for all in authority, that all who have power may use it with imagination and consideration for others. We pray for world leaders, and for each other in our own areas of influence and responsibility.

Lord, in your mercy:
Hear our prayer.

Lord Christ, you came that we should have fullness of life. We thank you for the life of this city, and our local community. We pray for all who are celebrating tonight in churches, pubs, clubs and at home. We pray that all of us, wherever we are, precious to you even when we don't respond to your love, will know your stillness at the heart of our festivities, and be touched by your redeeming love.

Lord, in your mercy:
Hear our prayer.

Lord, you came to bring healing and wholeness. We pray for all who suffer. As we give thanks for our families and friends, we pray for those for whom Christmas is difficult: those who will wake to another day of loneliness or pain; those whose celebration has been marred by the death of a loved one, or the disappearance of a member of their family.

In a moment of quiet, we bring our own needs into your healing presence.

Lord, in your mercy:
Hear our prayer.

Whatever lies ahead of us, may we always hear the echo of the angels' song, and help others to hear it too.

Merciful Father, accept these prayers for the sake of your Son, our Saviour Jesus Christ. **Amen.**

At the turn of the year

'New beginnings are always delightful, the threshold is the place to pause.' So said Robert Louis Stevenson. I'm not sure I fully agree with him. New beginnings, full of promise though they may be, are often close to endings which may have been painful. New beginnings always mean change, and there is something in all of us that makes us want to hold on to old, familiar, comfortable things. There may be quite a few of us who were given new slippers for Christmas, who are keeping them for best for the time being – they're too good for doing the housework or the gardening in: thinly disguised excuses for hanging on to the old.

But the threshold is the place to pause, yes. Thresholds are places of promise. In biblical terms they mark off something holy, a place where God is. We stand at the beginning of a year, a year where we shall find God. We don't have to take God with us into the new year, God takes us with him. That's what Christmas is about. Emmanuel, God with us. We don't have to cling on to Christmas, for Christmas is never over, God is with us.

Just before Christmas, the children came forward at the end of one service to report on their morning's activities. They had been thinking about the Christmas story, and some of the words it introduces us to. One of the words was 'Emmanuel'.

'What does that word mean?' asked the vicar.

There was a long pause, then a little boy said, 'I love you.'

That's not the official theologian's answer, but he'd gone right to the heart of it. 'I love you.' What we take with us into the new year, as reassurance and also as challenge, is the unfailing love of God. God's love isn't always comfortable. It doesn't always make things right for us. It doesn't mean we won't suffer, or find the world a difficult place to live in. God's love means that God is with us, right in the pain and the mess as well as the joy and the laughter. Christmas will never be over, it is always just beginning.

Pause at the threshold, and remember that God's love is new every morning: words worth pondering daily as we discover the riches and marvels of that love.

Epiphany

Picture the scene: a room with a large dining table. Three men in sumptuous flowing robes are watching a fourth man, obviously a servant, laying the table. Through a window, which by its shape tells us that this is a scene from the East, you can see a couple approaching in the distance, pushing a buggy with a child in it. One of the men explains the situation to the servant, who is looking a bit puzzled: 'You see, last year we went to them, so this year they are coming to us.'

I admire the skill of cartoonists, who with a few strokes of the pen and some well-chosen words can make a comment about our human condition, and at the same time make us think about deeper truths.

Over the last few years, cartoonists have provided some interesting springboards for thought about this Epiphany story. The one I have just described latches on to a perennial anxiety about where parts of a family spend Christmas, and whose turn it is to be host. With luck, we can laugh about it. But the deep truth about Jesus spending Christmas with us is that he comes every year, and stays with us all the time. So the real question is not about whose turn it is, but about how we are going to respond to this amazing generosity of God in giving himself to us.

The Wise Men in the story responded by offering gifts to the Christ-child. Another cartoon shows them having a conversation with each other. Two of them are holding the traditional gifts, the third is holding an envelope. In response to their concerned looks, he says, 'Yes, I know. But a token is so much lighter.' Will our response to God be a token gesture? Or will we offer something precious? And what precious thing have we got anyway? We need to be wary about using this story as if it's a prelude to a stewardship campaign – dig a little deeper into your pocket. It's more profound than that. The most precious thing we have is ourself. That is what God longs for us to give him.

We perhaps don't always think of ourselves as precious: we are quite good at putting ourselves down. But the gifts the Wise Men brought are our gifts too. Each of us is precious to God – in God's eyes each of us is pure gold. We may have to dig deep to find it, but that is God's truth about each one of us. Offer the frankincense of worship, and as we attend prayerfully to God, and learn more about God and ourselves, we recognize God's truth about us: 'You are precious in my sight, and honoured, and I love you' (Isaiah 43.4).

That truth about being precious will be tested with the myrrh of suffering – all around us, and perhaps touching us more personally too. Faithfulness to God's love is part of our response. As the carol puts it:

> What can I give him,
>   Poor as I am?
> If I were a shepherd
>   I would bring a lamb;
> If I were a wise man
>   I would do my part;
> Yet what I can I give him –
>   Give my heart.

That is a response to God not just for Epiphany, but for every day. Another cartoon takes us into the vestry, where the vicar is holding open a cupboard door. At his feet, the tiny crib figures process past him and the caption reads, 'So it was back into the vestry cupboard for another year.'

46

Will that be how we deal with Christmas too? Has the celebration made any difference to us? The commercial world has moved on, Christmas has been put away, hot cross buns are on sale. But Christmas isn't over. God is with us every day, the baby grows into adulthood if we will let him, and he challenges us to recognize him and respond to him in our daily lives.

Eucharistic Prayer for Epiphany

(The words at the Sanctus and at the end of the prayer come from the hymn 'Holy, holy, holy is the Lord')

Father of all blessings, we give you thanks and praise
for Jesus the Light of the world, the light that
no darkness can overpower;
we thank you that you have called us from darkness
to walk in his light;
we thank you for the insight of the Wise Men,
who by their gifts showed us
that all life is gift;
with them, and angels and archangels
and all who live in light,
we praise you, singing:
Holy, holy, holy is the Lord,
holy is the Lord God almighty, *(repeat)*
who was, and is, and is to come,
holy, holy, holy is the Lord.

Accept our praises now, Lord God,
as we remember Jesus,
who, on the night before he died,
took bread and wine, gave you thanks
and offered them to his friends, saying,
'This is my body, this is my blood.
Eat and drink to remember me.'

Come freshly to us now, Lord God,
as we offer you our lives.
Renew in us your gifts:
the gold of our potential,
the incense of our prayers and aspirations,
the myrrh of healing for our pain;
feed us and nourish us,

that we may grow in the life of Christ;
fill us with your Spirit
that we may overflow with your love,
and transform the world with your glory:
Glory, glory, glory to the Lord,
glory to the Lord God almighty, *(repeat)*
who was, and is, and is to come,
glory, glory, glory to the Lord.

Candlemas – Presentation of Christ in the Temple

The story of the Presentation of Christ told in Luke's Gospel (Luke 2.22-38), is one in which Anna and Simeon have a senior moment to die for – they are privileged to see the one who is to be the Saviour of the world.

Usually when we talk about having a senior moment, it's a rather rueful reference to memory failure. It's one of the kinder ways in which we refer to the business of growing older. Our society isn't always as kind when old age is under discussion. There are hints that old people pose a problem: pension funds won't last because old people are living longer; there are concerns about funding care for those who are unable to look after themselves, or finding people to do the caring.

This gospel story is about two old people who show some of the positive attributes of old age. They represent wisdom and simplicity, and offer us some helpful ideas about using our later years.

First, it's worth thinking about wisdom. There are others in the Christmas story, those visitors from the East who play a much more prominent part, whom we call wise. But a more accurate name for the Wise Men is 'Magi', marking them out as scientists of their time, discovering the secrets of the stars. Their 'wisdom' was perhaps more the cleverness of people who had a lot of knowledge in their heads, rather than the wisdom of the heart which brings insight into human behaviour. When you think about it, the Magi caused quite a lot of trouble with their cleverness, by jumping to conclusions about where the one who was to be the King of the Jews would be found. It's reasonable to think first of the ruler's palace: but such a birth would only be the cause of rejoicing if the child were the first-born. Herod already had a family which was torn apart by jealousies and intrigues. If the Magi had researched more widely, they would have discovered how much the Jews hated Herod and all he stood for. Then they might have approached their search for the new-born king rather differently, and avoided the problem that Herod could only deal with by murder. It wasn't very clever, let alone wise, to go to Herod.

Matthew was not writing his Gospel to comment on the Magi's method of discovery, but to show how Old Testament prophecies about the Messiah coming for all nations were fulfilled by their arrival to pay homage. Luke makes the same point about the Messiah being for all, when Simeon, in his recognition of Jesus, speaks of him in words that echo a prophecy of Isaiah: a light to lighten the Gentiles, as well as being the glory of God's people, Israel (Isaiah 49.6).

Simeon and Anna display the wisdom which begins with attentiveness to God and God's word. 'The fear of the Lord is the beginning of wisdom (Ecclesiasticus 1 .14).

'Fear', not in the sense of being afraid, but having a proper respect and reverence. Simeon and Anna recognize the significance of what is going on around them because they had waited, alert and hopeful, for the fulfilment of their longing. *Their* longing belonged to their circumstances, people of God oppressed, as they saw it, by a foreign power, longing for the promised Saviour who would set them free. They were not put off by the setbacks their people had experienced – they kept their vision alive, trusting that God would not let them down. They gave practical expression to their hope by being faithful to their religious observance. So they were there when

Mary and Joseph brought Jesus to the Temple, and they had eyes to see the promise in this child. They were realistic enough also to say that there would be no easy ride for child or parents in bringing that promise to fruition. I'm sure Mary remembered Simeon's words about a sword piercing her soul, as she watched her son grow up.

Simeon and Anna were old, and probably in the eyes of those around didn't achieve very much. But age isn't a time for productivity, it's the time for fruitfulness, a much longer-term result of growth. It's the stage when the wisdom we have acquired over the years can be harvested and shared.

Wisdom begins with attentiveness to God in prayer and worship, and alertness to the signs of God's coming in daily life. And wisdom grows when we give ourselves time to reflect, and give God a chance to reveal truth to us. Simeon and Anna took time – time to stand on the edge of the mystery of life and wonder at it, just as children do. Jesus said we need to become like children. People often talk about second childhood as a time of diminishment, and sadly, in our imperfect world, it can be. But let's not forget the good things about having a childlike attitude – perhaps the fact that grandparents and grandchildren enjoy life together can teach us something about that kind of simplicity.

So, time to explore the mystery of life, and time to explore the mystery of God. People used to talk about 'making their soul' in the last stages of life – learning to pray, to love, to be content, to enjoy beauty. We may not understand the mystery any more clearly, or find the answers to all our questions. But we may find that some of our questions don't matter all that much in the end. All that matters is that we are loved by God with a love that never fails. That's not to deny the difficulties and challenges of life, but to take hold of a very important resource our faith gives: 'It is better to light a candle,' as the Chinese proverb puts it, 'than to curse the darkness.'

Age does not have to mean diminishment. There may well be constraints: stiff joints, failing sight, a less reliable memory. There will be things we have to let go of – not always easy. And the last letting go happens when we die. Our society regards death as a failure, something to be avoided at all costs. But we can't avoid it for ever: and Christians have something very important to say about death. Perhaps we could begin to think about death as the last gift God will give us in this life, the gift that will take us into his fuller presence. Simeon seems to have felt something of that – he was ready to die. We don't know whether he died that day, or after an interval. We don't have to go out and seek death – but we do need to think about it, and learn that God's love will hold us through that experience too.

Candlemas is sometimes spoken of as the day when the Church's year changes direction. We stop looking back to Christmas, and begin to look forward to Lent and Good Friday and Easter. It's the growing time of the year, a season that will offer us plenty of opportunity to practise and grow in wisdom, so that, like Anna and Simeon, we recognize the moments of God's coming, and rejoice in God's love every day.

Eucharistic Prayer for Candlemas

Father of light, we give you thanks and praise
through Jesus Christ your Son, our Lord,
the light of the world
which no darkness can overcome.
We praise you that you have called us
from darkness to live in Christ's light.
With angels and archangels,
and all who are in that light, we praise you, singing:
Holy, holy, holy Lord,
God of light and love,
heaven and earth are full of your glory,
all praise to your name.

Come freshly to us now, Lord God.
Kindle again the light of your love
in our hearts, as we remember Jesus,
who, on the night before he died,
took bread and wine, blessed them
and gave them to his friends, saying,
'This is my body, this is my blood.
Eat and drink to remember me.'

Pour out your Holy Spirit, Lord,
set us on fire,
burn from us all that dims your light;
kindle an answering flame in lives around,
that darkness may be driven back,
and the whole world
come to live in your light.
For you are the God in whom is no darkness.
To you be praise and glory for ever. **Amen.**

Section 2

Lent to Pentecost

Thinking about Lent

'Most people think that behaviour matters and prayer helps it. The truth is that prayer matters, and behaviour tests it' (Archbishop William Temple).[1]

Fifty years or so ago, at each of the weekly confirmation classes I attended, the vicar read some verses from Philippians 3. In the Authorised Version, just about the only version available at the time, the words weren't very exciting. But they stayed with me, surfacing from time to time, and coming to life anew as different NT translations appeared: 'I want to know Christ and the power of his resurrection' (Philippians 3.10). On good days, when I'm asked what I really, really want, I know that's my answer: to know Christ, to be open to receive the gift of the risen life, to live it to God's glory and the benefit of my fellow humans.

Not all days are like that, though. There are all kinds of things that distract me from that focus. Paul knew about that too, and wrote about our need for discipline as an athlete needs to keep in training. Lent comes as a timely reminder, so I shall select one of my self-indulgences and attempt to show it who's mistress. But Lent isn't primarily a time for self-improvement, although that may be a spin-off. It is a time to grow, and my real aim, as it has been for some years, is to *do* less, and to *be* more; to spend more time doing nothing, being still, listening, looking, waiting in expectancy for God. And that kind of prayerfulness doesn't only operate in the times we label prayer, nor does it stop with the end of Lent, but grows in the whole of life, through Easter and beyond. It's another way of expressing what the Benedictines call conversion of life: a steady, continual turning to focus on God, opening up to God's Spirit, so that Christ can live his risen life in us.

Quite a challenge. And responding to it will keep me going for the rest of my life, let alone my Lents. But Lent comes to remind us to make space, paradoxically, to work at doing nothing, to make ourselves available to receive God's gift of life. For it is all gift. The risen life is not something I can achieve by my efforts, nor is it something I can do better than anyone else. We are not in competition over this, as we sometimes are over our Lenten discipline (is it more merit-worthy to give up chocolate or alcohol?). Receiving the gift of life means letting God free me to be 'God's work of art' (another phrase from Paul in Ephesians 2.10, brought to life this time by the Jerusalem Bible); it is coming to know deep down that I am precious in God's sight, and honoured, and loved (Isaiah 43.4). My response will be tested out in engagement with life, as I seek to enable others to receive God's gift, with all that implies of involvement with issues of social concern.

For me the question is not so much how I can best use Lent, but how I can best let God use it in me.

Note

1. See note 1 to 'Thinking About Prayer' in Section 1, p. 15.

Eucharistic Prayer for Lent

Lord God,
you fill us with longing for your presence,
yet require us to live with a sense of your absence.
Open our ears to hear the echo of your praise,
and tune our voices to sing your song,
as with angels and archangels,
and people of faith on different paths, we sing:
Holy, holy, holy Lord
God of life and love,
heaven and earth are full of your glory,
all praise to your name.

Come to us now, Lord God,
as we remember Jesus, who,
on the night before he died,
took bread and wine, blessed them
and gave them to his friends, saying,
'This is my body, this is my blood.
Eat and drink to remember me.'

Lord God, you have drawn us together
on the way of the cross,
and illumined our path
by the insights of others;
Come freshly to us, loving God,
with your disturbing power;
and as we receive this gift
of the life of your Son,
give us the courage to stay with
the discomfort of your call, and
satisfy our longing to be
in harmony with your will.

**Draw us to deeper commitment
to each other and to you,
that we may live to your glory
and sing to your praise all our days. Amen.**

Mothering Sunday
– say it with flowers

Mothering Sunday is a good occasion to think about the nature of God – for, as Julian of Norwich said in the fourteenth century, 'as truly as God is our Father, so also is God our Mother'.

People sometimes think that feminine imagery for God is very new, but it goes way back to some of the early books of the Bible. What about 'The eternal God is your refuge, and underneath are the everlasting arms' (Deuteronomy 33.27 NIV), or 'Can a woman forget her nursing child, or show no compassion for the child of her womb?' (Isaiah 49.15)? The prophet Hosea described the way God cared for his people in a very maternal way. 'It was I who taught Ephraim to walk, I took them up in my arms, but they did not know that I healed them. I led them with cords of human kindness, with the bands of love. I was to them like those who lift infants to their cheeks. I bent down to them and fed them' (Hosea 11.3-4).

We don't have to start calling God 'Mother' – that isn't necessarily any more helpful than 'Father'. But it is worth noting that there is this element in the biblical tradition, and it has been picked up by people in the centuries since.

So how can we respond to this God who is mother and father and so much else besides? Today, perhaps, we could say it with flowers.

How on earth can we do that? No floral delivery system has a way to cope with it! But we do talk about offering ourselves to God. I don't suppose you have ever thought of yourself as a flower, even though flower allusions abound in our language: we talk about being as 'fresh as a daisy', or we describe someone as being 'a shrinking violet'. People are sometimes 'prickly'.

But when you think about it, what kind of flower are you? Are you like a camellia, rather startlingly beautiful? Or like rosemary, starting to bloom right at the beginning of your life, and continuing year on year? Are you one of those plants that doesn't flower often? Or one that props others up? Are you a plant with rather insignificant flowers, but always there in the background to help others give of their best? Do you fill the world with fragrance, or give flavour to life?

Are you one of the plants that bring hope in the dark days of winter? Some plants are very beautiful when their flowers are dead – some people come into their own at the end of their life.

Sometimes we put a single flower into a vase and enjoy its beauty. At other times, we put many different varieties together in an arrangement. There is an important place for our individual response to God, but when we come together as a church we discover new things about ourselves as we relate to each other as well as to God. Like a flower arrangement, we can bring out the best in each other, and complement and support each other.

On our own perhaps we don't look very exciting – that doesn't mean we don't have our own beauty – but put with others, the ones who are a bit shy can find support, and those who are rather exotic can lend their colour and perfume to the more retiring. Even those who are prickly can be a great support to those who are fragile.

So we can give God quite a bouquet – and if we listen carefully, we'll hear God say, as every mother does, 'Thank you, dear, that's lovely!'

(One way of developing this idea is to accompany the words with some flower arranging, or to produce an arrangement that has been prepared earlier. This can be incorporated into the offertory. In one church, at the end of the service, the arrangement was given to the vicar, so that he could enjoy it during the week, and pray for his people too. The idea has also been used in one session of a Quiet Day. It could be followed by a session on being chosen. See the Quiet Day material in Section 3, pp. 151-56.)

Palm Sunday

I wonder what the donkey made of it all? Donkeys play quite a significant part in the stories of the Bible. They do the donkey-work, quite literally, and they were highly prized, especially the females. I don't think they were ever sacrificed – perhaps they were more valuable alive. For example, there was a donkey who spoke: Balaam's ass. She saw what was going on – more than the boss did, in fact, and eventually spoke to draw his attention to the presence of an angel. (Read her story in Numbers 22 – 24.) A donkey also carried Jesus invisibly to Bethlehem – perhaps he was present at his birth?

Another donkey, today's, carried Jesus publicly into Jerusalem. I wonder where she was at the end of the week. Was she tethered somewhere near the cross, with her foal? Why remember all these donkeys? I want to suggest that we are very like them. No offence! I don't just mean that we share their stubbornness and need a lot of coaxing sometimes; or that we always get lumbered with the donkey-work; or that we all behave like silly asses sometimes. All these are true in some measure. But we share something else that is much more important. Nearly all donkeys bear the mark of a cross on their backs. We carry the mark of the cross too, given us in baptism.

So what do these donkeys tell us about discipleship?

They remind us that we always carry Jesus invisibly, like Mary's donkey, wherever we go. Every day Christ is carried into his city, into his world, by us. As St Theresa said, 'Christ has no body now on earth but ours, no hands but ours, no feet but ours. Ours are the feet on which he is to go about doing good, ours the eyes through which he is to look with compassion on the world, ours the hands with which he is to bless us now.' So on the days when we feel we're carrying the world on our shoulders, we need to remember that we are also bearing Christ to meet the world's pain and give people life.

There are times when, like Balaam's ass, we shall see things that others can't or won't see. Then we have to do something about it. Balaam's ass tried first of all to draw the boss's attention to the demands of God, the angel standing in the way, and got pretty rough treatment for her trouble. But then God gave her words to say, and Balaam began to take God seriously.

Being a Christian, being outspoken for God, isn't always going to be easy or pleasant. Balaam was trying to maintain his reputation, and wasn't keen on anything standing in his way. We shall find ourselves challenging important people and vested interests – that can be very hard, like crucifixion.

Today's donkey reminds us that when we go with Christ, there are no promises about easy rides. We know, however, which she did not, that at the end of the suffering, after the death, there was resurrection. We know that Christ has promised to keep us company, but as we carry him with us in the world, he won't avoid confrontation, or allow us to. 'In the world', he said, 'you will have tribulation.' We know that, from personal experience, and from sharing in the pain of the world, as people starve, exploit and kill each other. We shall have to hang on with some of the donkey's stubbornness to the belief that Christ really has overcome the evil in the world, and that we shall share that victory.

So here we are, at the beginning of Holy Week, armed with our crosses, ready to ride out again with

Jesus, to be his donkeys as he goes the way of his cross. God grant that we will be faithful, so that, accompanying him to the cross, we may also know in ourselves the power of his resurrection.

Maundy Thursday

Throughout the Christian world, on this day, people will be having their feet washed, re-enacting what Jesus did with his disciples the night before he was crucified. And all of them, I expect, will have washed their feet before they go to the ceremony.

They will have done it partly out of concern for the one doing the washing – we all know the jokes about smelly feet. They will have done it to protect themselves, too – feet are such personal things; we don't like people messing about with them. Feet are very vulnerable: they get blistered and calloused, corns and bunions make them painful – and anyone getting near our feet might tickle them. We'd be helpless, at their mercy.

We understand all that. And we understand Peter's reluctance to have his feet washed too – not for any of our reasons – Peter, after all, like his friends, would have been used to having his feet washed. It was part of the normal courtesy of hospitality in a hot, dusty country, where guests were refreshed on arrival at their destination with water for footwashing. But this was different. This was Jesus, their leader, taking on a servant's role, doing a woman's work. And Peter's instinctive reaction was to say, 'Surely it should be the other way round, me kneeling before you?' Jesus meets his objection by saying, 'Let me serve you. Let me meet you as you are, and minister to you.'

It's hard to let others minister to us. When Jesus said, 'It is more blessed to give than to receive' (Acts 20.35) he could have added, 'and easier,' too. Most of us are fiercely independent, and we have to learn the willingness to receive graciously. Otherwise, if we are always the ones who give, we diminish others by implying that they are the ones in need, while we are all right. Jesus didn't say, 'Go and wash *everyone else's* feet', he said, 'Wash *one another's* feet' (John 13.14). There has to be a mutuality of service. Jesus modelled that himself, when he let someone wash his feet. Remember the woman, emotional, over the top with her extravagance? (Luke 7.37-48). Scandalous, really, that she should think she had anything to give Jesus, especially in view of her background. But Jesus didn't refuse her ministrations — he knew that she needed to express deep gratitude for her acceptance, and for the forgiveness that had set her free.

So we have to learn to be on the receiving end, as well as doing the washing. Washing people's feet has nothing to do with making them pleasanter to be with. It has everything to do with making people feel welcome, loved and cared for.

And it is hard. People don't turn up on our doorstep with ready-washed feet. They come with dirty feet, feet misshapen by experience, blistered, smelly. And Jesus says that's where we have to get stuck in. It won't always, perhaps even often, be a physical soap and water job. But there will be times when we have the opportunity to minister to someone, to meet them at their point of need; not to make them more acceptable to us, but to help them live with themselves, to begin to understand what it means to be loved.

And if we don't do it? Well, have you noticed that there were two bowls of water called for that night? Jesus took his, filled it with water, and used it to wash feet (John 13.5). Symbol, he said, of love. Pilate sent for his and used it to wash his hands of responsibility (Matthew 27.24).

The bowls are constantly before us. Into which will we dip our hands?

Eucharistic Prayer for Maundy Thursday

God our Father,
we gather on this night
in praise and gratitude
that you come to us in love,
and that in your Son, Jesus Christ,
you have shown us
how your love must be shared
by honouring and serving others.
With angels and archangels
and all who have tried
to respond to you in humble service,
we worship you, saying:
Holy, holy, holy Lord,
vulnerable God,
heaven and earth are
full of your glory.

Come to us now, Lord God,
as we meet to break bread
and share Christ's life,
 who, on the night before he died
took bread and wine, blessed them
and gave them to his friends, saying,
'This is my body, given for you.
This is my blood, shed for you.
Do this to remember me.'

Pour out your Spirit on us now, Lord God,
as we bring before you these gifts
of bread and wine, and remember
Christ's sacrifice made once for all
upon the cross.

Nourish us with his life
that we may live and grow in him.

Give us his spirit of service
that we may love as he loves us.

Take from us all fear that the
cost will be too great:
Keep us faithful, keep us joyful;
for you are the God who delights in us,
and in Christ has called us your friends.

To you, Father, Son and Holy Spirit
be praise and glory, world without end. **Amen.**

Good Friday

These three meditations, lasting one, two and three hours to cater for most requirements, are suitable either for congregational use, or for individuals wanting material to use on their own. They are all based on sections lasting 20 minutes, and are intended to encourage periods of reflection within each section.

In the two- and three-hour services, it is not expected that the Bible passages should be read aloud – they are there for people to use if they find them helpful, so Bibles should be available.

I have found it useful to provide an outline of whichever set of material I have been using, giving times, topics for each section, Bible references and hymn numbers, so that announcements can be kept to a minimum. It is helpful to have this information to give to people who come in part the way through the service, to help them orientate themselves.

The guiding principle behind these acts of worship is to leave plenty of time for personal reflection. People very quickly get used to silences lasting between five and ten minutes, even if it is not their normal practice.

The sacred tree – one hour

I

Sing: 'Bless the Lord, my soul' (Taizé)

Bless the Lord, my soul, and bless God's holy name,
Bless the Lord, my soul, who leads me into life.

Introduction

American Indians tell the story of a sacred tree, which the Creator has planted. Under it all the people of the earth may gather, and find healing, power, wisdom and security. The roots of this tree spread deep into mother earth, its branches reach up like praying hands to father sky. The fruits of this tree are all the good things the Creator has given to his people: love, compassion, generosity, patience, wisdom, justice, courage, respect, humility, and many other wonderful gifts.

Their ancient teachers taught that the life of the tree is the life of the people. If the people wander far from the tree, if they forget to seek nourishment from its fruit, or if they turn against the tree, and try to destroy it, great sorrow will come to them. Many will become sick at heart, they will cease to dream and see visions, they will begin to quarrel among themselves over worthless things. They will be unable to tell the truth, and deal with each other honestly. They will forget how to survive in their own land. Their lives will become filled with gloom. Little by little, they will poison themselves and all they touch.

But the tree would never die. As long as the tree is alive, the people would live, and one day they would come to their senses, and begin to search for the tree and its truth. Wise elders and leaders have preserved knowledge of the tree, and they will guide anyone who is sincerely seeking for it.

We have come to spend time at the foot of our sacred tree, the cross. There is a medieval poem called *The Dream of the Rood*, which describes the crucifixion from the point of view of the cross, the tree that was cut down and used as a shameful support for a dying man. But the tree says that, much to his surprise, he wasn't the support for a dead weight, but rather the mount for a triumphant Christ, who rode him like a victor in battle. Here is a modern version of the same idea.

Poem: Rood-tree

I might have been his cradle,
Rocking him, folding
Securely against harm.
I could have been a ship,
Turning my sturdy timbers
To the wind, keeping him
Safe from storm.

Instead they used me as
His cross.

No infant rages rocked the
Cradle tree, or storm lashed ship
Such as unleashed on me
That day. Shock waves of hatred
Crashed against me, bearing
On me through his body
Weight of world's pain,
Weight of his agony;
Wringing from him
Drop by drop,
'Why, God, you too?'

No comforting protection
Could I offer, or deliverance;
Only support, his mainstay in distress.

But did I hold him, or did he
With strength of purpose lovingly
Embrace his work of suffering,
Stretched on my arms?

They say it was a tree whose fruit
Brought sorrow to the world.
The fruit I bore,
Though seeming shame,
They call salvation.

My glory was it then,
To be his tree.

The cross is not ashamed to be associated with Christ, and nor should we, marked with the sign of the cross, be ashamed to bear him with us in our world.

Silence, ending with the prayer:

May we, signed with the sign of the cross, never be ashamed to confess the faith of Christ crucified, for the sake of him who died and lives for the world, Jesus Christ. **Amen.**

Hymn: 'When I survey the wondrous cross'

II

In the old Genesis story, it was the fruit of a tree which brought our downfall. Was that an apple tree? But there were two trees mentioned in that story, and God didn't forbid the fruit of both of them.

Poem: Two trees (Genesis 2.9)

God did not say
'You must not eat
Fruit of the Tree of Life.'
But burdened by guilt
At tasting the forbidden fruit
Of the other tree, our energy
Is spent in dealing with our
Dreadful knowledge of
Good and evil.

And all the while,
The Tree of Life offers us
Nourishment.

Eat its fruit, and live.

When Adam and Eve left the Garden, the way to the tree of life was guarded, so that they couldn't get back to it. But between that time and this Christ has opened the way to life, and he invites us to feed on the life that he gives.

Another medieval poem, 'Jesus Christ the apple tree', talks about Jesus as a tree.

Think of all the things trees provide: protection and shelter, warmth, a meeting place, nourishment, healing. Jesus is all these things.

Sing or listen to: Elizabeth Poston's setting of 'Jesus Christ the apple tree'.

Jesus offers us new life, so in the silence now, we ponder on this gift.

Fragment

Feed on him in your hearts, digest his power;
Let his life slow release itself into your blood,
Stream through your senses, energise your thoughts.
Recall his presence thankfully,
A constant savouring.

Silence, ending with the prayer:

Father, we give you thanks that the tree of shame was made the tree of glory, and that where life was lost, there life has been restored, in Jesus Christ our Lord. **Amen.**

III

And what of us?

The Letter to the Ephesians offers us tree pictures too.

Reading: Ephesians 3.14-19

The imagery of the tree is strong: we in our turn are to be trees, nourishing the hidden life of our roots through prayer, Bible reading, worship; and letting the visible part of our life offer to the world all that Christ the tree offers us.

Poem: Christ the tree

Deep-rooted in the
Love of God the Father,
Moving, responding to
The Spirit's power;

Drawing all people
By your ageless
Wisdom, giving
To all who come
Healing and strength;
Life bursting forth,
Disturbing, powerful;
Cut down,
But bearing fruit.

Here I will rest,
And wait until sap rises,
Your life in mine,
My resurrection.

Our roots need to go deep. Roots are powerful, and what roots us in the love of God is prayer.

Poem: Prayer tree

Prayer gives us rootedness,
Reaching out,
Discovering in darkness
Sources of nourishment;
Pushing with patient insistence
Against obstacles;
Drawing from strange places
Strength for life that
Grows in light;
Holding us as we bend,
And when we break, offering
Hope, that from the
Unimaginable dark,
New shoots will spring.

We need to stay close to Christ the tree, but the nourishment Christ gives has to bear fruit: it is not just for our benefit, but for the sake of the world.

Silence, ending with the prayer:

Lord God, nourish us so that we bear fruit for you and offer healing and peace to all around, for the sake of your Son, who was lifted up so that the world might be saved.

Hymn: 'There in God's garden stands the tree of wisdom'

Blessing

Seen by the cross – two hours

Hymn: 'We sing the praise of him who died'

'Seen by the cross' is a title which can be taken two ways. There were people close to the cross as Jesus was crucified – Mary his mother, the beloved disciple, the soldiers and the centurion. A little further off, perhaps wanting to get closer, but not allowed any nearer, the women, among them Mary Magdalene, and Peter, unless he was so heartbroken at the way things had turned out that he couldn't bear to be there. And the cross itself, if it could speak, would have noted their presence. Perhaps it would also have noted the absence of two people who had been prominent in the run-up to the crucifixion, but who had chosen to go a different way.

Judas and Pilate may seem a strange pair to link together, for their allegiance lay in different directions. But both of them were driven by their own agenda, which in the end proved to be too strong to allow them to stay with Jesus.

Judas

Judas is thought to have been a Zealot, a member of a political party aiming at the overthrow of the Roman government. He couldn't wait for Jesus to get on with it. A few days before, it had seemed as though the moment had come: there was Jesus, entering Jerusalem in triumph – it could have happened then. Of course, it would have been better if Jesus had ridden into the city on a horse, like a real conqueror, instead of looking a bit stupid on a donkey. But the people were with him: 'Hosanna, save us now,' they had yelled. And then what happened? Endless talk, upsetting people in the Temple. He'd miss his chance if he wasn't careful. Worse, the way he was going on, he'd get himself killed for the wrong reason. Perhaps if he was put in a position where he'd have to fight or die, he would get on with it. So the plans were laid. The religious leaders didn't care what Judas' motives were, so long as he told them where they could find Jesus away from the crowds. A small reward – he could have held out for a big one, but it wasn't the money, it was the Cause that mattered.

And then the awful realization that he'd got it wrong. His attempts to rescue the situation failed. And he felt that his life was not worth living (Matthew 26.14-16, 47-49, 27.3-10).

Pilate

Pilate was in a different position. He was running scared. It had been a difficult job from the beginning. Whatever pleasure he might have had from his promotion to governorship was spoilt by fear that he might not be man enough for the job. He'd decided right at the start that he would show the Jews who was boss. He marched into Jerusalem to take up his post, with the Roman eagle carried proudly at the head of the cavalcade. Redecoration of his new home included some of the same emblems. The Jews threatened to report him to his superiors for provoking them by bringing emblems of a foreign god into their holy city. When he showed no signs of giving in, they demonstrated outside his palace. He was no match for a chanting mob, and the decorations were removed.

He'd trodden warily ever since, and mostly the province had been quiet and peaceful. But now there was another threat, the Jesus business. Pilate couldn't understand what the fuss was about – the fellow seemed harmless enough, even positively good. Pilate had heard about his care for people and his healing power. There didn't seem to be any hint of his rebelling against Caesar – in fact, when he'd been challenged Jesus had quite clearly said that people ought to give Caesar his due.

So when the Jewish leaders came and asked him to get rid of Jesus, his first instinct was to have nothing to do with it. He tried very hard to avoid sending Jesus to his death – but when he heard the words 'If you let this man go you are not Caesar's friend', his blood ran cold. 'Not Caesar's friend' meant he was Caesar's enemy, and that spelt death for him. So he called for a bowl of water, and washed his hands of the whole affair (Matthew 27.11-26).

But someone else had taken a bowl of water earlier that night, and washed his disciples' feet, a symbol of the loving service he wanted his followers to engage in (John 13.1-20). Those two bowls represent the choice always before us. Will we follow Christ's example, throw in our lot with him? Or will we let a different agenda run our lives? The bowls are always before us. Into which will we dip our hands?

Silence

Prayer

Lord God,
draw us ever closer to you.
When we are faced with difficult choices,
help us to seek your will;
when we are frightened
for our personal safety,
give us courage;
when we are challenged with others' need,
give us compassion;
for the sake of Jesus Christ our Lord. **Amen.**

1.20 p.m. Hymn: 'O word of pity for our pardon pleading'

Peter

Perhaps we identify more easily with Peter than we do with Judas and Pilate. After all, he didn't make a choice to force Jesus' hand, or wash his hands of any responsibility for what happened to Jesus. He was caught out by weakness, rather than making a deliberate choice. Perhaps that's what happens to us too.

Peter had always been an enthusiastic follower, even if he hadn't always got things right. He sometimes blurted words out without thinking first – sometimes he got it gloriously right, like the time he said that Jesus was the Christ, the Messiah. And sometimes he got it horribly wrong – almost immediately after that great confession of faith, he got a stinging rebuke from Jesus when he said that the Messiah didn't need to suffer as Jesus said he would. But he'd learnt that Jesus didn't hold it against people when they got things wrong, if they were genuinely trying. Jesus hadn't said, 'You're not the rock I thought you were.' He'd gone on putting his faith in Peter, taking him with James and John on some significant occasions, like the Transfiguration, and into the Garden of Gethsemane; calming things down when Peter's enthusiasm got a bit out of hand, as it did when he attacked one of the soldiers in the Garden.

But what happened after the arrest had brought Peter to despair. Jesus had warned them that they would be put to a severe test that night. And Peter had been so sure that he wouldn't let Jesus down – 'Even if the rest deny you, I won't,' he'd said. And

Jesus had said that before cock-crow, Peter would have denied him three times.

We know what happened. Peter followed at a distance when Jesus was led off, and in those long dark hours three times he was approached in the courtyard, and three times he denied being anything to do with Jesus.

At the point when Jesus was led out to be crucified, through the courtyard where Peter was trying to keep warm by the fire, the cock crowed. Luke tells us that Jesus turned and looked at Peter – and Peter remembered how Jesus had warned him that this would happen. And he went out and wept bitterly (Luke 22.24-34, 54-62).

That response of Peter's tells us something about Jesus' look. If it had been the kind of look that says, 'I told you so', Peter's response would probably have been to get defensive – 'What did you expect? I didn't think you'd go to those lengths. I've got a wife and family to support – I couldn't put my life on the line.' But that wasn't his response. He wept bitterly. The look must surely have been a look of love, that said, 'I know you, Peter – and you are still the rock on which I will build.' Such love and understanding would move anyone to tears.

So would Peter have been there at the cross? I think he would. I think he had begun to get a glimmer of the truth that Jesus reinforced for him after the resurrection: that nothing we do can stop God loving us. And we can be there too, longing to love, not always getting things right, but beginning to realize the love of God which nothing can destroy.

Silence

Prayer

In our sight we do not stand,
in God's sight we do not fall.
Both these insights are true,
but the greater belongs to God.
Merciful God, help us to grasp this truth,
and hold it fast, for the sake of your Son,
Jesus Christ. **Amen.**

(Based on words from Julian of Norwich)

1.40 p.m. Hymn: 'Just as I am, without one plea'

Mary

Standing by the cross was his mother. How do we identify with her?

Medieval devotion and catholic piety have conspired to put her on a pedestal – an unattainable figure of virtue who isn't like us at all.

You always appear too good to be true, Mary.
We've pictured you always serene,
Never exasperated by a fractious child,
Apparently having no feelings.

But surely that initial Yes came
From a moment of overwhelming terror,
And the birth tore you to the core?
Didn't he ever cry, that baby,
Give you sleepless nights?
Didn't he irritate you,
That precocious son
Dismissing your anxiety with
Didn't you know? And later
That wounding question
Who is my mother?
My mother would have told him ....
Perhaps you did too,
But it wasn't recorded.

(From 'Get real')

There are many indications in the gospels that Mary was baffled by her son. Pondering on the events surrounding his birth may have been a source of comfort to her – but may have increased her bewilderment too. Jesus had been ordinary enough as a boy, learning the values of God's kingdom at Mary's knee and Joseph's bench. There was that puzzling event in the Temple when he was 12, when he seemed to be laying claim to another source of authority (Luke 2.41-51). But they had weathered that as a family, and Jesus had remained at home with them until the moment came for him to begin his public work. Then it seemed that he was abandoning his family to establish another set of relationships with all those who were intent on doing God's will. 'Who is my mother, and who are my brothers? ... For whoever does the will of my Father in heaven is my brother and sister and mother' (Matthew 12.49-50). Perhaps Mary remembered then the words of Simeon when her baby was six weeks old: 'This child is destined for the falling and rising of many in Israel, and to be a sign that will be opposed so that the inner thoughts of many will be revealed – and a sword will pierce your own soul too' (Luke 2.34-35).

I don't think that sword waited until the crucifixion to pierce her heart – there were other moments when it must have felt that a knife was twisting within her.

Mary and the rest of the family seem to have followed Jesus' activities, even if they weren't part of the inner circle of his followers. It must have been very hard for Mary to see her son running into opposition, apparently asking for trouble. Bittersweet the realization that all his words and actions echoed her Magnificat, as he taught and preached the kingdom values she must have taught him.

And then the hardest thing of all, to be there watching him die, not even being able to touch him to bring him comfort. Surely that wouldn't have been a Mary serene in her grief as artists portray her. Much more like those ravaged faces we see on our screens, raging at the senseless killing of the innocent.

It's in our rage and pain that we can stand at the cross, too, and begin to feel the saving power of one who comes to us with wounded hands, to cradle us in love.

Silence

Prayer

Lord, with wounded hands we pray that you will cradle your world in your love. Heal your suffering people, and restore your exploited creation, that we may all learn to honour one another, and live in wholeness to your glory. **Amen.**

2.00 p.m. Hymn: 'O sacred head'

The beloved disciple

'Jesus saw his mother, and the disciple whom he loved standing beside her' (John 19.26-27).

The beloved disciple appears only in John's Gospel – at least, he's only described in that way by John. We don't know who he is, but he is clearly very close to Jesus.

He appears first at the account of the Last Supper, where he is described as lying close to the breast of Jesus (John 13.23-25). Peter asked him to find out who Jesus had been talking about as the betrayer. The beloved disciple, in the intimacy of that closeness, asked, 'Lord, who is it?'

We see him at the cross, and then again at the resurrection, when in response to Mary Magdalene bringing the news that the Lord's body is not in the tomb, he runs with Peter, reaches the tomb first but does not go in, leaving Peter to do that. But it is the beloved disciple who saw and believed (John 20.1-8).

He is also the subject of Peter's question, after Peter's restoration when he is called again to follow Jesus. Peter sees the beloved disciple and asks, 'What about him?' And Jesus says in effect, 'That's a matter for him and me. You take responsibility for your own calling' (John 21.20-23).

So we really don't know much about him, except that he was very close to Jesus, close enough at times to hear his heart beat. And he stayed close, right up to the cross, entering into the pain and suffering of his Lord. Because he was there, he was entrusted with the care of Jesus' mother, and because he had been close, he understood, in a way that Peter didn't at first, what the victory of the cross over sin and death was. He saw beneath the surface, and believed.

So who was he? It doesn't matter. He was the beloved disciple, one whom Jesus loved. He was each one of us, loved as we are. He gives us the clue to discipleship: that it begins and is undergirded by staying very close to Jesus; that it will take us to the heart of suffering; that it gives us a responsibility for others, and that it gives us insights into the nature of eternal life, that quality of life that transcends death and keeps us close to the heartbeat of God.

Silence

Prayer

God, of your goodness, give us yourself, for if we ask anything that is less than can do you full worship, we shall always be in want. Only in you we have all. Amen.

(from Julian of Norwich)

2.20 p.m. Hymn: 'My God, I love thee'

Mary Magdalene

Who was she? There's confusion about her identity, because several stories in the gospels could be about her. There's a story Luke tells (Luke 7.36-50) of a woman who was a sinner who burst into tears over Jesus, anointed him with precious ointment and dried his feet with her hair. Jesus recognized her penitence, her desire to change. He drew attention to the fact that a realization of forgiveness brings a response of love, and sends her on her way a new woman. John told of a similar event (John 12.1-8) and identified the woman with Mary of Bethany. So she had a name.

Luke also tells us about the women who supported Jesus, among them Mary Magdalene from whom seven devils were cast out (Luke 8.1-3). There has been much speculation about those devils: in the history of the Christian Church, the area of human life about which people seem to have had the most hang-ups is sexual desire and relationships. So it was a very short step to say that her problem lay in her sexual behaviour – she must have been a prostitute. It is more likely that people possessed with demons were suffering from what we have learned to call mental illness – they were ill, not evil.

Artists have often portrayed Mary Magdalene weeping, and that gave rise to our word maudlin –

weak, sentimental, tearful – like some people are when they've had too much to drink. And there was a kind of social work called Magdalen care up to the mid-nineteenth century, primarily providing for women and girls in moral danger, some of whom were prostitutes.

So mention of Mary Magdalene would cause people to give each other a nudge and a wink, and say she was no better than she should be. But when we look at the evidence in the gospels, all that we can say is that she came from Magdala, a commercial town with a big fishing fleet on the shores of Lake Gennesaret; she was healed by Jesus – whatever the seven devils represented was put to rights, and her response was to support Jesus with her friendship. She became the leader of a group of women who contributed from their wealth to keep the Jesus movement on its feet. Far from being maudlin, she was strong, someone with leadership qualities, who stayed faithful right to the end; there at the cross, going to the burial place to do what was necessary to ensure that her Lord had a proper burial (John19.25, 20.1-8). Perhaps it doesn't matter who she was – she was like all of us, a mixture:

Damaged and healed,
Longing to be loved
And struggling to relate;
Passionate and reserved
By turns, working out
Costly discipleship.

(From 'Known by Name')

The important moment for her was when she was called by name. And that's our important moment, too, when with all our confusions and questions about our identity, we realize that we are known by name and loved by God. And as Mary was sent out to spread the good news, so are we. For being known and loved by God doesn't bring us into a cosy relationship, it is the basis of our witness to the love of God for everyone.

Silence

Prayer

My God, I desire to love thee
with all my heart
which thou madest for thyself;
with all my mind
which only thou canst satisfy;
with all my soul,
which longs to soar to thee;
with all my strength, my feeble strength,
which shrinks before so great a task,
and yet can choose nought else
but spend itself in loving thee.

Claim thou my heart,
fill thou my mind,
uplift my soul and
reinforce my strength,
that where I fail,
thou mayest succeed in me,
and make me love thee perfectly.

(W.H. Frere)

2.40 p.m. Hymn: 'My God accept my heart this day'

The cross

If the cross could speak, what story would it tell? Right at the centre of the picture, was it an instrument of shame and degradation, or a place of victory?

Depictions of the cross in art and literature have followed the insights of theology. In early centuries, artists rarely focused on the suffering of Christ, rather on his victory. The earliest known depiction of the crucifixion, from Rome in about 420, shows Christ standing upright on the cross, his eyes open, his body unmarked by suffering, a victor over death. It was not until some centuries later, when theology moved the emphasis from the work of God the Father to the suffering of God the Son, that the man of sorrows became the model for the figure on the cross.

There is an Anglo-Saxon poem that expresses a strong belief that the cross was about glory. Called *The Dream of the Rood*, the poem describes how the dreamer heard the cross describe what the experience of bearing the crucified Christ was like. In it the cross speaks of the way it was set in place, prepared to bear the weight of the one being crucified, only to find that he came to the cross not as an abject victim, but as a warrior, mounting the cross and fighting for the salvation of humankind. Undoubtedly, crucifixion was a shameful death in the eyes of Jews and Romans alike. But to the eye of faith, the tree of shame became the tree of glory, and where life was lost, there life has been restored.

We are called not just to stand at the cross, but to take up our cross – to witness to the victory won on that Good Friday. We trivialize the idea of taking up the cross when we use the phrase to describe putting up with things we don't like. 'It's the cross I have to bear,' we say, in the tone of voice that is meant to evoke sympathy for our plight. But that is self-indulgence. Taking up the cross has a sharper edge to it – and we don't have to manufacture our cross. Perhaps we would be closer to the truth if we were to think of it as being true to the cross with which we were signed at baptism. Taking up our cross means being true to that sign, bearing Christ with us wherever we go. Bearing witness to our belief that God really has overcome the evil in the world – always looking for God in the intractable areas of suffering and exploitation and grief, as well as rejoicing in God's presence where we experience life. Taking up our cross will mean challenging the forces that exploit or destroy, affirming the people who build up and encourage. It's not a path that will bring us instant popularity or success – for Jesus it meant crucifixion. But as Julian of Norwich said, 'He did not say you will not be tested, he said you will not be overcome.'

Silence

Prayer

We adore you, O Christ, and we bless you, because by your cross you have redeemed the world. **Amen.**

Hymn: 'When I survey the wondrous cross'

2.55 p.m. Conclusion

We stand at the foot of the cross, where this great work of salvation has been unfolding.

The last word is with the centurion, who had watched all this going on too, and found himself at something of a crossroads (Mark 15.39).

Poem: Crossroads

I cursed my luck, on duty in that heat:
The flies, the blood, the stench of death.
It was the loneliest place I've ever known,
Standing beside that cross. The crowds,
Hurling abuse, engulfed me with their hate;
Had he no friends? Standing not far away,

The women had more courage than the men,
But even his God, it seemed, had left him.
I've seen some crucifixions in my time,
But never one like this: the victim
More concerned for others than himself,
Asking forgiveness for his murderers.
And then that awful darkness, when
The world died with him, and the cry that
Pierced the darkness pierced me too.
Did he say, 'Finished'? The way I feel
It's only just begun.

Dismissal

And now we go out to continue the story.

In the name of Christ. Amen.

Prayer at the cross – three hours

In this three hours, we shall follow Jesus through the week leading up to the crucifixion, and look at prayer in the light of his experience. After the introduction, in each 20 minute section, there will be a period of silence for reflection and prayer. The words from a Psalm or one of the Prophets, printed in the order of service, may help you to focus on the theme. Each period of silence will end with a poem or a prayer, and a hymn.

We begin where Jesus began, as we sing the hymn: 'Ride on, ride on in majesty'.

Prayer as encounter

Jesus rides into Jerusalem: Mark 11.1-11.

On Palm Sunday, Jesus rode into his city, and the people knew exactly what he had come for. 'Save us now,' they shouted, 'Hosanna to the Son of David!'

But they misread the signs. Jesus was riding a donkey, not a horse; he'd come in humility, not earthly power. And he didn't do what people expected. He didn't start a revolt, he went to the Temple and looked around.

We come to prayer, often, thinking we know what it's about. We lay before God our hopes, our fears, our demands and requirements; we say, 'Your will be done', and often mean 'Lord, do it my way.' But prayer is always a searching experience. We read in 1 Corinthians 3.16, 'Do you not know that you are God's temple, and that God's Spirit dwells in you?' Prayer is an engagement on God's terms, not ours; we come in response to his call, not to do him a favour. And when we draw near in prayer, he will look around us, his temples.

Metropolitan Anthony Bloom reminded us that this God with whom we have to do is not a tame cat, but a tiger. Before God, all we can do is stand, or kneel, or fall on our faces in awe and wonder.

To ponder in the stillness

O come, let us worship and bow down,
Let us kneel before the LORD, our Maker!
For he is our God.

(Psalm 95.6-7)

Silence

Prayer: Lord God, you reveal yourself in simple ways, yet you are greater by far than our imagining. We praise you for your great glory. **Amen.**

12.20 p.m. Hymn: 'My God, how wonderful thou art'

The prayer of anger

The cleansing of the Temple: Mark 11.15-17.

Palm Sunday over, there were mixed feelings about what Jesus had come to do. The next day, Jesus came back to the Temple and drove out the money-changers, and those buying and selling animals for sacrifice, with some violence. You remember the layout of the Temple: a central Holy of Holies, which only the High Priest could enter, and then only once a year; the Holy Place, where the priests carried out some of their duties; the Court of the Israelites, for the men; the Court of Women, and outside, and beyond all that, the Court of the Gentiles. A place where you had your place, and knew your place. There were rules about what had to happen. Ordinary coins had on them the image of the Emperor, and had to be changed into Temple money with all the dissatisfaction that we experience with exchange rates. Animals for sacrifice had to be without blemish, and the easiest way to ensure that was to acquire them on the spot. All that went on in the court of the Gentiles. There was no peace for prayer there, and the Gentiles could go no further on pain of death. However we try to soften it, the description of this event shows Jesus angry – angry at the way the 'in' crowd excluded the outsiders. 'Is it not written, "My house shall be called a house of prayer for all nations"?' By siting the money-changing and the sales in the court of the Gentiles, the only part of the Temple non-Jews could go into, all non-Jews were prevented from joining in the prayer without noisy distractions.

We don't like to think of Jesus being angry – we find him easier to deal with if he is gentle, meek and mild. Perhaps part of our difficulty with an angry Jesus is that we don't know how to deal with our own anger. We are perhaps frightened by the violence we know within ourselves – perhaps we have been taught from an early age that anger is sinful. And so, often, it is. But at times, anger is God's spur to right wrongs, relieve oppression, see justice done.

If we have begun our prayer by attending to God and worshipping him in his greatness, we have to learn to continue it by looking at the world through his eyes, and recognizing that part of our prayer has to be action which will, as Amos put it, enable 'justice [to] roll down like waters, and righteousness like an ever-flowing stream' (Amos 5.24).

To ponder in the stillness

What does the Lord require of you but to do justice, and to love kindness, and to walk humbly with your God?   (Micah 6.8)

Silence

Poem: Temple cleansing

Sometimes the only right response is
Anger. Not dull resentment,
Poisoning all it touches, or
Bitterness that taints the memory,
But a clean cutting edge, that
Lances festering grievances,
Releasing energy to fight;
The fuel of passion that
Challenges evils
Outwardly observed
Or known within.
Such anger is not sin.

12.40 p.m. Hymn: 'What does the Lord require for praise and offering', or 'The kingdom of God is justice and joy'

Wrestling with hard questions

Jesus in the Temple: Mark 11.27-33; 12.13-34; 41-44.

Jesus went back to Bethany each night in the early part of the week, but the third day in Holy Week saw Jesus back in the Temple, wrestling with questions about authority, life and death, loyalty to God. One after another the questions came.

First, from the Pharisees – by whose authority? If you can discredit someone, you don't have to listen. And then a couple of trick questions.

Taxation – is it lawful? 'Bring me a coin.' That would have involved a trip back to the money-changers. Jesus wasn't going to be caught out by having a coin in his possession. Whose image is on it? Then give him his due. But give God what is his too.

Then the Sadducees, who didn't believe in life after death, came up with an old chestnut, the one about the woman who married seven brothers in turn. In the resurrection, whose wife would she be?

Each time, Jesus turned the question back, with 'What do you think?' He always does that, he's not one for giving easy answers. Work it out for yourselves, he says. If you've got ears, hear. If you've got minds, think.

We sometimes treat prayer as though it's a magic formula: apply it in the right way, pray properly, and we'll get the answers. But it's not quite like that. Jesus isn't the answer, he's the question, probing our hearts and minds: what do you really think about life and its purpose, how much do you really want to give yourself to God?

Amidst all the questioning, perhaps it's one of the other people Jesus saw that day who gives us the clue, the widow who gave all that she had. Learning what is God's will is rooted in attending to God. The answers to our hard questions emerge from the kind of commitment that the widow had.

To ponder in the stillness

For God alone my soul waits in silence.

(Psalm 62.1)

Silence

Prayer

Lord Jesus Christ, alive and at large in the world,
Help me to follow and find you there today,
In the places where I work, meet people,
Spend money and make plans.
Take me as a disciple of your kingdom, to see through your eyes,

To hear the questions you are asking,
To welcome all others with your trust and truth,
And to change the things that contradict God's love
By the power of the cross, and the freedom of your
Spirit.

(John V. Taylor, from *A Matter of Life and Death*)

1.00 p.m. Hymn: 'Be thou my vision'

Prayer as resting

Jesus with his friends: Mark 14.3-9.

On 'Wednesday', Jesus appears to have spent time with his friends in Bethany, and allowed himself to be cared for, made a fuss of by the woman who anointed him. Perhaps we are a bit embarrassed that Jesus lets himself be ministered to. Perhaps we're not very good at letting others minister to us. 'Oh, you shouldn't have,' we say. 'You shouldn't have spent that much on me ....' One of the disciples said that. 'Fancy spending that much on him.' And these were his friends! We're not very good at accepting. We're not very good at resting either. There's something in our British character that makes us feel we've always got to be on the go. Kipling's version of the Protestant work ethic, in his poem 'If', says it for us:

> If you can fill the unforgiving minute
> With sixty seconds' worth of distance run,
> Yours is the world and everything that's in it

(we won't dwell on the last line, about 'being a man, my son'!).

Yours is the world ... Jesus said, 'For what will it profit them if they gain the whole world but forfeit their life?' (Matthew 16.26). The Bible is full of invitations to come apart and rest, be still, and know God.

To ponder in the stillness

In returning and rest you shall be saved;
in quietness and trust shall be your strength.

(Isaiah 30.15)

Silence

There's a hymn which begins, 'Father, hear the prayer
we offer, not for ease that prayer shall be.' One
response to that could be the poem:

Poem: The prayer we offer

Not for ease? Why not?
What's wrong with ease?
For most of us the
Problem is not self-indulgence,
But that we allow ourselves too little.
Prohibitions, counsels of perfection
Drive us and load us up with guilt.

Time enough for courageous living
And all that rock-smiting.
Let's rest and wander in green pastures
When we find them, make the space
To let ourselves be loved;
Build up our strength
And grow in confidence;
Drink living water springing in
Great fountains;
Feed on the Bread of Life which
Satisfies.

Then we shall have provision
For the journey, and at last
Arrive, not too unpractised
In the art of resting
In his presence.

1.20 p.m. Hymn: 'Dear Lord and Father of mankind'

Sharing in God's life

The Last Supper: John 13.1-9; Mark 14.22-24.

Maundy Thursday, New Commandment day.

We find it hard to let others care for us. We find it harder to rest with God. One reason for this is that we don't really believe that God loves us. We can't allow ourselves to think we are lovable.

At the beginning of the passage from John, Jesus washed the disciples' feet. Picture the scene: reclining at the table, perhaps they don't at first realize what Jesus is doing. And then it dawns on them. Our feet are very personal things – they carry the marks of our life in very particular ways, and we don't like people playing with them. The thought of someone else washing our feet, let alone our Lord, is almost too much – and anyway, they might tickle.

So, like Peter, we back off –

What, let you wash my feet?
Shouldn't it be the other way,
Me kneeling before you?

(From 'Maundy Thursday')

The feeling that we'd be at Christ's mercy if we let him get that close makes us keep him at arm's length, at least.

But first the footwashing, and then the gift of Christ's life as he gives his body and blood, are invitations to us to open ourselves to the love of God, let him love us into wholeness, let him re-form his likeness in us, who were made in his image. We are very special to God.

To ponder in the stillness

... you are precious in my sight, and honoured,
and I love you.

(Isaiah 43.4)

Silence

Poem: Love

Love bade me welcome; yet my soul drew back,
　　　　Guilty of dust and sin.
But quick-eyed Love, observing me grow slack
　　　　From my first entrance in,
Drew nearer to me, sweetly questioning
　　　　If I lacked anything.

'A guest,' I answered, 'worthy to be here':
　　　　Love said, 'You shall be he.'
'I, the unkind, ungrateful? Ah, my dear,
　　　　I cannot look on Thee.'
Love took my hand, and smiling did reply,
　　　　'Who made the eyes but I?'

'Truth, Lord; but I have marr'd them; let my shame
　　　　Go where it doth deserve.'
'And know you not,' says Love, 'Who bore the blame?'
　　　　'My dear, then I will serve.'
'You must sit down,' says Love, 'and taste My meat.'
　　　　So I did sit and eat.

(George Herbert)

1.40 p.m. Hymn: 'Just as I am, without one plea'

Prayer in pain

The Garden of Gethsemane: Luke 22.39-46.

After the brief respite in Bethany, the tension is really beginning to build up now.

If it is hard to let God love us, and learn to rest in his presence, it is even harder to love God when life goes bad on us. At times we are overwhelmed with suffering – the suffering of the world, our own personal pain, physical, mental, emotional, spiritual …. 'What have I done to deserve this, why me?' we cry. 'God, where are you? Why don't you do something, put things right?'

And when we feel let down, betrayed, and cry out in our anger and bewilderment, Jesus in Gethsemane shows us where God is. Right there, suffering alongside us. 'Father, let this cup pass from me, yet not my will, but thine, be done.' God's will is not that people should suffer, but that people should live in wholeness and peace. Jesus absorbed all the hatred and pain without hitting back, so that that greater will of God could have its chance.

Prayer is not always sweet conversation – there are times when all we can do is speak through gritted teeth …. Perhaps this silence won't be very comfortable, but we have to stay with it, as Jesus stayed with it in Gethsemane.

To ponder in the stillness

Save me, O God,
for the waters have come up to my neck.
I sink in deep mire, where there is no foothold;
I have come into deep waters, and the flood sweeps
over me.

(Psalm 69.1-2)

Silence

Poem: Psalm 84

Use this?
You must be joking.
Who could find comfort
In such bitter water?
Rather, let this cup
Pass from me,
This cannot be your will.
Why should life be
Like this?
Why me?

Why not?

And anyway,
There's not much choice.
It's this or nothing.
Use it for a well,
And see what happens.

In the heat of struggle
It is not sweetness which refreshes,
But the astringent bitterness
Which sets the teeth on edge.
Drink deep, and find
Mysterious refreshment.

2.00 p.m. Hymn: 'Have faith in God, my heart'

Prayer at the cross

Jesus is crucified: Luke 23.33-34.

Now we stand at the foot of the cross. What do we make of it?

This is the point where prayer really searches us out, because Jesus said, 'If you want to be my disciple, this is where you must be – take up your cross and follow.'

We sometimes talk about unpleasant or difficult tasks or relationships as 'the cross we have to bear'. That trivializes the cross, and has more to do with Victorian piety than the gospel. The cross means being willing to join Jesus in acknowledging the hatred and evil that is all around us, and within us, too, when we are honest about it, and refusing to contribute to it or add to its power.

This is where we learn about forgiveness, about its cost. This is where to the outsider the Christian gospel looks like folly – but to those who believe, there is a touch of glory.

The motivation for taking up the cross is thanksgiving, not as punishment. It is our response to the amazing, forgiving love of God.

To ponder in the stillness

Bless the LORD, O my soul, and all that is within me, bless his holy name.
Bless the LORD, O my soul, and do not forget all his benefits –
who forgives all your iniquity, who heals all your diseases.

(Psalm 103.1-4)

Silence

Poem: Rood-tree

I might have been his cradle,
Rocking him, folding
Securely against harm.
I could have been a ship,
Turning my sturdy timbers
To the wind, keeping him
Safe from storm.

Instead, they used me as
His cross.
No infant rages rocked the
Cradle tree, or storm lashed ship
Such as unleashed on me
That day. Shock waves of hatred
Crashed against me, bearing
On me through his body
Weight of world's pain,
Weight of his agony;
Wringing from him
Drop by drop,
'Why, God, you too?'

No comforting protection
Could I offer, or deliverance;
Only support, his mainstay in distress.

But did I hold him, or did he
With strength of purpose lovingly
Embrace his work of suffering,
Stretched on my arms?

They say it was a tree whose fruit
Brought sorrow to the world.
The fruit I bore,
Though seeming shame,
They call salvation.

My glory was it then
To be his tree.

2.20 p.m. Hymn: 'When I survey the wondrous cross'

Prayer in darkness

'My God, My God, why have you forsaken me?' Matthew 27.46.

Here, at the heart of the mystery, is a sense of total loss. People have sometimes suggested that Jesus was saying Psalm 22, knowing that all would be well in the end. It seems to me that it is unlikely that in the extremity of pain and exhaustion, Jesus would be remembering anything as long as that Psalm. Once again, as with the thought of Jesus being angry, which we considered in connection with the cleansing of the Temple, perhaps we are saying more about ourselves than about Jesus. We don't want to let Jesus bear the agony of feeling abandoned by God, because we can't contemplate the possibility of that sort of pain.

But if that cry of desolation means anything to us at all, it must mean real desolation, desolation mirrored in the record of the event by the darkness that covered the earth. It means that we must not be surprised if what we experience at times, perhaps much of the time, is a feeling of God's absence, rather than a sense of his presence. Perhaps in retrospect, when we have been through a period of desolation, we can finish the Psalm, and say of the dark times, 'Yes, God was there too.' But in the middle of desolation, all we can do is hang on. Our prayer may not get further than, 'My God' – but that prayer is perhaps the most profound we shall ever pray.

To ponder in the stillness

My God, my God, why have you forsaken me?
Why are you so far from helping me, from the words
of my groaning?
O my God, I cry by day, but you do not answer;
and by night, but find no rest.

(Psalm 22.1-2)

Silence

Prayer (from Psalm 130)

Out of the deep we call to you, O Lord,
Lord, hear our prayer. **Amen.**

2.40 p.m. Hymn: 'O sacred head'

The prayer of trust

It is finished: John 19.30; Luke 23.46.

Our last session, at the foot of the cross, brings us to a settled place – the place where after all the agony and struggle, Jesus can say, 'It is finished.'

Not a thankful, 'That's over', but a recognition that he has accomplished what had to be done. In that knowledge, he can rest, trusting in God, 'Father, into your hands I commend my spirit.'

We have to learn that trust, that total surrender. We have to learn to trust, even when we're being crucified.

To ponder in the stillness

You who live in the shelter of the Most High,
who abide in the shadow of the Almighty,
will say to the LORD, 'My refuge and my fortress;
my God, in whom I trust.'

(Psalm 91.1-2)

Silence

Prayer

Keep us, good Lord,
under the shadow of your mercy
and, as you have bound us to yourself in love,
leave us not who call upon your name,
and grant us your salvation
made known in Jesus Christ our Lord. Amen.

2.56 p.m. Hymn: 'My song is love unknown' or 'Praise for the mighty love'

Conclusion

So we stand at the foot of the cross, where the battle has been lost and won. Humanly speaking, the last word lies with the centurion ...

Poem: Crossroads

I cursed my luck, on duty in that heat:
The flies, the blood, the stench of death.
It was the loneliest place I've ever known,
Standing beside that cross. The crowds,
Hurling abuse, engulfed me with their hate;
Had he no friends? Standing not far away,
The women had more courage than the men,
But even his God, it seemed, had left him.
I've seen some crucifixions in my time,
But never one like this: the victim
More concerned for others than himself,
Asking forgiveness for his murderers.
And then that awful darkness, when
The world died with him, and the cry that
Pierced the darkness pierced me too.
Did he say, 'Finished'? The way I feel
It's only just begun.

Dismissal

And now we go out to continue the story.

In the name of Christ. Amen.

A simple vigil on Easter Eve

After lighting the new fire, and the Paschal candle, process into the church, lighting individual candles on the way.

Sing: 'The Lord is my light, my light and salvation, In God I trust, in God I trust.' (Taizé)

When all the candles are lit, the ministry of the word begins:

Introduction

The first time God spoke, at creation, God said, 'Let there be light.' Tonight we come to give thanks for Jesus, the Light of the world, which the darkness of sin and death have not been able to overcome.

It is a long story, the story of our salvation. Year by year, we read in Scripture how God created men and women in his image, to live by his laws. We read how human beings chose to go their own way, with the consequent loss of their closeness to God and to each other.

We hear how God called his people with yearning love, again and again; how they responded and fell away. And God never let go. Sometimes, to save his people from disaster, God performed mighty acts, as with Noah, or at the parting of the waters of the Red Sea. Sometimes, individual prophets called the people back to God. At times, it seemed as though God's purpose would never be fulfilled, as his people were overpowered by foreign nations, and finally taken into exile. But there, at one of their lowest points, God spoke again with a message of new life.

Reading: Ezekiel 37.1-14.

Let us pause to reflect on God's faithfulness.

Silence, ending with

For all his mighty acts, and for his hidden mercies:
God's name be praised.

For keeping the word of hope alive through prophets and leaders:
God's name be praised.

For the promise of new life, when all seems hopeless and dead:
God's name be praised.

Hymn: 'The God of Abraham praise'

Restoration to their land did not bring total restoration of their relationship with God, though, and succeeding generations followed the pattern of turning to God and turning away again. Finally, as words did not seem to get through to his people, God performed his mighty act of deliverance in Jesus Christ. His life was an embodiment of God's word of love. His teaching and manner of life went right to the heart of what it means to live in close relationship with God. A tremendous struggle against the powers of darkness was focused on him, and, at one point, darkness appeared to have won. But out of the darkness came the voice of Jesus from the cross – 'It is finished. It is accomplished.'

On the third day, God's people began to understand what that cry from the cross meant, when Jesus, the Light which could not be overcome, appeared among them, risen from the dead.

Gospel: John 20.1-8.

Hymn: 'Now the green blade rises'

And the story goes on, for we have been called out of darkness to live in God's light. That is what our baptism means, and so it is most appropriate that on this night of thanksgiving, we should renew our vows.

Renewal of baptismal vows.

Prayers, ending with the Lord's Prayer.

Blessing

May the risen Lord Jesus watch over us and renew us as he renews the whole of creation. May our hearts and lives echo his love. **Amen.**

Sing: 'Kindle a flame' (Iona song)

Together we say

**Lord Christ, set us on fire,
burn from us all that dims your light;
kindle an answering flame in lives around,
that darkness may be driven back
and glory stream into your world
transforming it with light. Amen.**

A reflection for Easter Eve

At Christmas you probably heard the reading from St John's Gospel that describes the birth of Jesus in two ways. John called Jesus the Word of God made flesh, coming to live with us. He also spoke about the Light that enlightens everyone coming into the world, a light that shines in the darkness, and that cannot be extinguished (John 1.1-14).

When Jesus was preaching, you remember that he said, 'I am the light of the world. Whoever follows me will never walk in darkness, but will have the light of life' (John 8.12).

The events we were remembering in the early part of the week, and especially on Good Friday, showed how people tried very hard to extinguish the light. At one point it even looked as though they had succeeded, as darkness covered the earth, and Jesus died on the cross.

But the resurrection of Jesus, which we are beginning to celebrate, showed us that God isn't so easily defeated, and our Easter candle is our proclamation that Jesus is alive, and is the light for all people.

But Jesus didn't only say, 'I am the light of the world.' He also said to his followers, '*You* are the light of the world' ... Let your light shine ... so that [people] may give glory to your Father in heaven' (Matthew 5.14-16). Paul picked up this idea, too, when he wrote to the Christians at Ephesus (Ephesians 5.8-14): 'Once you were darkness, but now in the Lord you are light.' The Church reminds us of that in baptism, too, when the person who has been baptized is given a candle, and told to 'Shine as a light in the world, to the glory of God the Father'.

To take that to ourselves again, I invite you to give the light of Christ to each other as we light our candles from the light of the Paschal candle, saying as we pass the light on, 'The light of Christ'.

When the candles are lit

Often on Easter Eve, people renew their baptismal vows. These promises are about inviting Christ into our lives to drive out the darkness of sin, so that we can show Christ's light to the world.

We are invited to renew our promises now ....

or

I invite you to join in the prayer:

Lord Christ, set us on fire,
burn from us all that dims your light;
kindle an answering flame in lives around,
that darkness may be driven back,
and glory stream into this world,
transforming it with light. Amen.

We sing: 'The Spirit lives to set us free,
Walk, walk in the light'

At the end of the evening, take your candle with you, and light it again, tomorrow, and in the weeks ahead.

A story of new life for Easter Day

Henry and Henrietta were two tiny, wriggly caterpillars. They lived on a bush in a beautiful garden, and every morning when they woke up, they began to eat the leaves of the bush. Occasionally, when they paused for a rest, they looked around them, and noticed that there were other creatures in the garden, too. Some wriggled along like they did, some hopped, some walked, some flew. Some were ugly, some were rather ordinary, some were beautiful to look at. But the most beautiful of all were the butterflies.

'Oh,' thought Henrietta, 'if only I could be a butterfly, beautiful and free.' She hadn't realized that she had spoken aloud, until a voice spoke from a nearby flower: 'You can be a butterfly, if you are willing to change.' Henrietta looked round to see who had spoken, and there, on the flower, rested a beautiful butterfly. 'I was like you once,' said the butterfly, gently fanning her wings, 'but I gave up being a wriggly caterpillar, so that I could become a butterfly, because that's what I was made for.'

'Is it hard?' asked Henrietta. 'Not very,' said the butterfly. When the time is right for you to start to change, you'll find that you can spin a cocoon to protect you while you grow. It's not hard, but you will feel as though you are dead for a while, until new life begins to stir.'

'Did you hear that?' Henrietta said to Henry. 'We can be beautiful, free butterflies.'

'Sounds a bit risky to me,' said Henry. 'I'm happy as I am, munching these leaves, and getting bigger and fatter. You do what you like, but I'm going to be the biggest and best caterpillar there has ever been.' And he went on eating.

Nothing Henrietta said could make him change his mind. She was sad about that, because she enjoyed his company, and would have liked to share this rather scary adventure with him.

Sure enough, one day Henrietta thought it was the right time to make a start. She discovered that, as the butterfly had said, two of her legs had a special ability to spin thread, and she began to cover her body with it, round and round, until nothing could be seen of her old caterpillar shape. It was very dark and a bit scary. She began to wonder if she'd done the right thing. Perhaps Henry had been right after all, and it would have been better to stay as a caterpillar, and try to be the biggest caterpillar there had ever been. But she'd done it now. She would never get out of this cocoon alive. She would never see Henry again.

But just as she reached the depths of despair, she began to feel something happening around her. Her cocoon was breaking open, light was coming in, and warmth. She began to stretch – and found that in the darkness she had grown wings. In the warmth of the sun, she began to move them up and down, and discovered that she could fly. 'It's true,' she shouted in delight, 'I'm a butterfly – I am beautiful – this is what I was meant to be.'

Meanwhile, Henry was very uncomfortable. His skin was tight, and he found it hard to move. He wished he'd never said he wanted to be the biggest and best caterpillar there ever was. And he was lonely without Henrietta, too – life didn't seem to make sense any more. He felt awful, and very sorry for himself.

But then he heard a voice that he knew, calling him. 'Henry!' He looked round, thinking that Henrietta had come back. But all he could see was a beautiful butterfly, gently fanning her wings beside him. 'Henry,' the voice said again. 'It's me, Henrietta.

It's true, it's worth the risk. Don't try and cling on to your old way of life. Come through the darkness, and join me in the light of this new life.'

So Henry had his chance after all, and he and Henrietta danced in sunlight for the rest of their lives.

We heard another story this morning when someone was told not to cling on to an old way of understanding: the story of Mary Magdalene in the garden, looking for the body of Jesus. She was told that she was looking for the wrong thing, because Jesus was not dead, but risen.

As we've followed Jesus from his entry into Jerusalem on Palm Sunday, through the growing tension of his encounters with various people in authority, as well as the illumination of his encounters with his followers, we've thought a lot during this week how we are continually being invited to let old ways die, so that new life can come. Everything led up to the cross on Good Friday, that very dark, scary place. And now this glorious day of the resurrection comes to us again, with the same message:

> If you have been raised with Christ, seek the things that are above, where Christ is, seated at the right hand of God. Set your minds on things that are above, not on things that are on earth. (Colossians 3.1-2)

Listen to Jesus saying
'Do not cling ....
Let me be bigger than your
Heart can hold.
Rise with me to a
Larger vision.'

('From Easter Morning')

The Lord is risen, he is risen indeed. Alleluia!

Eucharistic Prayer for Easter

Lord God,
through your Son, Jesus Christ,
you have renewed our hope
in life that cannot be destroyed by death.
We thank you for calling us
to witness to the resurrection:
Lord, keep us faithful.

With Mary Magdalene, Peter, John
and all who through the ages have believed
although they have not seen,
we join the angels and archangels
and all the company of heaven, as we sing:
Holy, holy, holy Lord,
God of life and love,
heaven and earth are full of your glory,
all praise to your name.

Accept our praises now, Lord God,
as we remember Jesus, who,
the night before he died,
took bread and wine, gave you thanks
and offered them to his friends, saying,
'This is my body, this is my blood.
Eat and drink to remember me.'

In joy and awe we stand before you,
and proclaim:
Dying he destroyed our death,
rising he restored our life.
Lord Jesus, come in glory.

Come freshly to us, living God:
open our eyes
that we may recognize you walking with us;

open our ears and our minds
that we may hear and understand;
open our hearts
that your love may flow through us
and bring the blessing of new life
to all we meet;
for you are the God who makes all things new.

Blessing and honour and glory and power
be yours for ever and ever. Amen.

Ascension Day

When I was a child, Ascension Day was always a special day, a holiday at the school I attended, a golden day, full of glory.

One day seems very much like another now, even Sunday can be spent just like the rest. Our sense of the rhythm of the year belonging to the Christian story has gradually been diminished. Public holidays have had a major shift ever since Harold Wilson's government moved the Whitsun holiday to the end of May, instead of celebrating it inconveniently as a movable feast attached to the Christian Pentecost, which, of course, depends on the date of Easter. Holiday has become a secular word, far removed from its origin in 'holy day'. But, however we spend it, Ascension Day is a special day in the Christian calendar, a day which marks the completion of the story of Jesus' earthly life, though not the end of his relationship with us.

The ascension is a puzzling event if we try to take it too literally. It is recorded in language which belongs to a different era, when people didn't understand the shape of the universe or, rather, thought it had a very clearly defined shape. The earth was flat, and surrounded by water. Over it the sky fitted like a dome, and above the dome was heaven where God was to be found. Two thousand years on, we've discovered a lot about our physical surroundings. We know that the sky isn't solid. Yuri Gagarin, the first Russian cosmonaut, told us that he didn't find God or heaven when he went into space. We know that the earth isn't flat – it's all much more complex than people ever imagined.

And language is complex too. We talk about things being 'up' or 'down' without giving the words any sense of direction. Each year at school, I 'went up' to a new class at the beginning of September. Sometimes that actually meant moving down a floor in the building. If we are 'put down' by someone, we are devalued, not moved a couple of feet lower. Our language in many ways reflects that old picture of the universe. So moving on to something richer and fuller is symbolized by the word 'up'. And we are using language in that symbolic way when we talk about the ascension. Just as at Christmas we sang, 'He came down to earth from heaven, who is God and Lord of all', now at the ascension we sing about the completion of that earthly, incarnate life, and celebrate with our upbeat language (there we go again!) the lordship of Christ over all creation.

'Lord' is another word we have to work at – it doesn't sit comfortably with our twenty-first-century view of things. Some would like to get rid of lords altogether. But it goes further than a feeling that it's unfair to inherit power and land. We've spoilt the word and the concept by the way some of us 'lord it' over others. All through human history, people have misused their power and abused those whom they were supposed to protect.

But Jesus gave the word 'lord' a special meaning. He said to the disciples (Mark 10.42-45) 'You know that among the Gentiles those whom they recognize as their rulers lord it over them ... but it is not so among you ... whoever wishes to be first among you must be slave of all.' And he gave them a particular demonstration of what he meant when he washed their feet: 'You call me Teacher and Lord,' he said, 'and you are right, for that is what I am' (John 13.13), but I don't lord it over you, I respect you and accept you as you are, feet and all. And that is how you must treat one another. Real humility does not lie in thinking we are no good. It lies in looking at others and recognizing their value – we could even say 'looking up to them'.

Washing people's feet is not a way of making them more acceptable. It is a way of taking people as we find them, sore and weary or fresh and dancing, and seeking to serve them, whatever their need. It's not so much that we have something to give them, as recognizing that all our fellow humans are special to God, just as we are. Washing their feet, in whatever form that takes, will help them to realize that too.

We are always being asked to choose whether we will join Christ in service or not. The Lordship of Christ does not speak of a remote being, distant from all our concerns, but about an involved God who wants his kingdom to be established. God longs for justice where there is injustice, sufficiency where there is poverty, health where there is sickness, knowledge where there is ignorance. And we are the people he has called to work with him to bring his kingdom nearer.

If that seems a rather big undertaking, way beyond our grasp, remember the promise Jesus gave: 'You will receive power when the Holy Spirit has come upon you, and you will be my witnesses' (Acts 1.8) and 'I am sending upon you what my Father promised; so stay here in the city until you have been clothed with power from on high' (Luke 24.49).

So we're not expected to do God's work *for* him, but *with* him, in his strength, filled with his Spirit – a kind of divine job-share. May the Spirit open us up and transform us, so that we will be able to live the good news we have to share.

The Ascension and mission

'Go therefore and make disciples of all nations' (Matthew 28.19). At Ascensiontide it is hard to avoid thinking about the meaning of mission, because that is what the gospel calls us to. Our spiritual growth is not something we engage in for our own benefit, or so that people will think how wonderful we are. Our aim has to be that people will learn how wonderful God is in his transforming grace (Matthew 5.16). Although Matthew's Gospel was directed to Jewish people, he did not forget that the Jewish mission was to all the nations (Isaiah 49.6). At the beginning of the Gospel, the nations come to Christ, in the persons of the Magi. At the end, the disciples are sent out to all nations. The Church is to be the new Israel.

So we come to the question: 'What is mission?' And how do we do it? That command to go out and make disciples of all nations was the spur for missionary work throughout the centuries, and some of it was done from rather questionable motives – not all Church history bears too close an examination. In the nineteenth century, it was the driving force behind the work of missionary societies from this country, which sent people out to what they thought of as the benighted parts of the world, to bring people to the light. In the twentieth century, as the British Empire crumbled, questions began to be asked about how far spreading the Christian gospel had been part of Empire building, part of the package that imposed the British way of life, rather than a desire to help people see God as he is in Jesus. Christian mission must always be fuelled by that desire.

We are faced with real questions, though, about how we relate to people of different faith traditions. Attitudes have changed over the last 50 years or so, as we've learnt more about the ancient traditions of other cultures and learnt to respect them, and to appreciate the insights they have into the nature of God. This change is reflected sometimes in the hymns we sing, or don't sing. As a teenager I used to go to missionary meetings, where often one of the hymns chosen as part of the worship was 'From Greenland's icy mountains ...' which listed all the places where the light of Christ had never been seen, and contained the words, 'The heathen in his blindness bows down to wood and stone'. You won't find words like that in hymns now, even if you can find the hymns.

In the hymn, 'Thy kingdom come, O God', the words of one verse, 'O'er heathen lands afar, thick darkness broodeth yet', have been changed to 'O'er lands both near and far ...'. Thirty years ago when I was teaching in Sheffield, we sang the unreconstructed version – political correctness hadn't come into fashion then. I remember standing in church as we sang it, with my thoughts travelling about six miles to the outer city estate where I taught, an estate with huge problems caused by deprivation. The darkness seemed pretty impenetrable there. And in the school community there were two faith groups, some Christians fairly sure they were right, and a group of Muslim lads who put many Christians to shame by their steady witness to the importance of their faith. This was pointed up very sharply one year when Ramadan coincided with Lent in a very snowy February. As most of us, Christians and all, rushed towards hot chocolate and the KitKat machine at break-time, when the rule was that pupils had to go outside, the Muslims simply asked if they could be allowed to stay in the building because they found it hard to cope with the cold when they were fasting. They were fasting to show their love for God. How did the Christians show their love? It was quite a challenge.

When I came back to Southampton 25 years ago, I was involved with the early inter-faith explorations in the city, and I found myself challenged again by the experience of meeting people of different faiths – but this time on their own terms. Standing in the Hindu temple, looking at the images of the gods, all my colonial prejudices rose up – the heathen, blindness, bowing down to wood and stone. And then almost like a physical blow I was struck by the question: You say that you believe in one God, what does that mean? Could it be that God has different ways of revealing himself in different cultures? Sitting in a Sikh Gurdwara, where I didn't understand a word of what was going on, I had a strong sense that it was God who was being worshipped. Meeting Muslims in their place of worship wasn't possible then – they were a tiny community meeting in a house adapted for the purpose, and there was only room for the men to pray together. But we were invited to go to meet them out of worship hours, and we talked with one Muslim who said more than once that the purpose of our conversations must always be to make us better members of our own faith community.

It is not easy. When we hold convictions, they matter. But our convictions can be sharpened and deepened by exploring the convictions of others and offering them the insights of our own, not to demolish their arguments, but for mutual enrichment. For some people, truth is like a castle: once you have got into it, you are safe. But you have to defend it from attack and, in effect, it can become your prison. For other people, truth is more like a journey, with camps pitched along the way, where pilgrims meet each other and exchange ideas. This kind of exchange challenges us to discover what we really mean when we say, 'Jesus is Lord.'

One of the things I have realized is that we hear things in a certain way because we've always heard them that way. For example, an often-used text in inter-faith discussions is, 'No one comes to the Father but by me.' The emphasis is always put on *me*. Why should it not be on *Father*? There is nothing in the Greek from which that verse is translated to say where the emphasis should fall. And to emphasize 'Father' opens up other possibilities. John Hick put this helpfully when he wrote:

> No-one comes to the Father – that is to God as Father – except through Christ, in whom as Son the love of the Father is fully revealed. But millions of men and women may in Buddhism have come to God as release out of suffering into Nirvana; or in Islam to God as sovereign and holy will addressing the Arab peoples through Mohammed; or in Hinduism to God as many-sided source and meaning of life. And further, it may be that Christ (as personal love) is also present in these other religions, and their several awarenesses of God likewise present to some extent in Christianity.[1]

For Christians, the special uniqueness of Jesus is that he shows the character and nature of God the Father as only a Son can. He focuses all the other insights we have about the nature of God. But it is worth remembering that much of the proclamation in the New Testament is about the Christ who is to come – we haven't got all the truth in our grasp yet. I'm sure it's true that in Christ 'all the fullness of God was pleased to dwell' (Colossians 1.19). But I'm not sure we fully understand yet what that means.

The alternative to dialogue, the attempt to get to know and understand, is the fanaticism which tries to impose our way on others, the attitude which the 2004 Reith Lecturer, Wole Soyenka, described as the 'I'm right, you're dead' approach, with which we have become all too familiar.

Mission, the dialogue which includes listening, has to begin from the place of humility. That is what the incarnation demonstrated. Dialogue has to leave room for people to disagree without destroying each other. If we really believe there is one God, we have nothing to fear from people who understand God differently. God is much greater than any human, or religion, can comprehend, and God will draw people to respond to him in the ways he wants. Our job as Christians is to witness to how God is in Jesus, and we can leave the rest to God. We can trust the promise Jesus gave us: 'You will know the truth.' He didn't go on to say 'and the truth will keep you safe', but 'the truth will make you free' (John 8.32).

NOTE
1. Quoted by John Robinson in the chapter 'The Uniqueness of Christ' in his book *Truth is Two-Eyed*, Philadelphia, Westminster Press.

Pentecost

'What's going on?' That seems to have been the question on everyone's lips at Pentecost. The reason for the question is clear when we read the account of that day in Acts 2. The Christians were gathered together, and suddenly a violent wind swept through the house, and tongues of flame rested on each person there, and the Holy Spirit filled them. They were so excited that they spilled out into the street, talking at the tops of their voices. The extraordinary thing was that everyone who heard them understood as though it was their own language being spoken, whatever country they came from. 'What does it mean? What's going on?' they said.

Some people dismissed the whole affair as drunken revelry, but Peter brought them down to earth. Apart from the fact that it was the wrong time of day for drunkenness, he told the crowd that they ought to recognize that this was what was foretold by the prophets. He quoted one called Joel, who had said that God promised to pour out God's Spirit on everyone, young, old, male and female, and the result would be outward signs of excitement and disturbance, and inwardly the opening up of the possibility of salvation, of being changed (Joel 2. 28-32).

Peter could have pointed to other clues which were there in the events: the people who were wondering what was happening would all have known their scriptures. They would have known that the word for 'wind' or 'breath' was a word that also meant 'spirit'. They would have remembered that Ezekiel had seen the dry bones of the Jewish people revived by the Spirit of God (Ezekiel 37.1-14). They would have known, too, that fire was a sign of God's presence:

ever since the time that Moses heard God speaking from the middle of the burning bush, flame had carried that symbolism. But perhaps those people present at Pentecost were like us, knowing things in our heads, but a bit slow to make the connection between what we know intellectually, and what we experience.

So what was going on, and what might it mean for us today? We could perhaps pick up a different clue. John recalled at the beginning of his Gospel (John 3.1-8) how Jesus had said to Nicodemus, 'You must be born again, filled with God's Spirit.' Again, as with Hebrew, the Greek word for 'wind' is the same as that for 'spirit'. Jesus went on to talk about the mysterious way the wind operates, blowing where it wants to. We don't know where it has come from or where it is going. We may understand more about weather systems now than people in first-century Palestine, but we are no nearer to being able to control the wind. No more are we able to control God's Spirit.

Some of the things we say about the wind may help us to understand more about the way the Spirit of God will affect us. We talk about an idea or a person coming like a breath of fresh air: blowing away the cobwebs, clearing the air. So God's Spirit can set us free from habits and ways of thinking that keep us stuck, and prevent us from seeing straight. And we talk about 'the wind of change', too. That's more radical than simply feeling a breath of fresh air. It's the phrase that came into prominence in the 1960s, when the first signs appeared that apartheid in South Africa was beginning to crack up. And that process meant real upheaval, painful change which is still going on.

So, when Jesus said that the Spirit would come and lead us into truth (John 16.13), he was not just talking about the Spirit sorting out our muddled thinking. He was saying that there is real, hard work to be done. Repentance, turning round to face the truth, is costly. And the Spirit of God gives us the clarity to see, and the energy to do, what needs to be done.

For the other attribute of wind that can help us is its energy. We are getting used to the idea of wind-farms providing us with power. But the energy of the wind isn't just for work, the wind can set things dancing, too: it's there to be enjoyed and played with, especially if we're lucky enough to have a kite to fly. The Spirit of God can set *us* dancing, too, filling us with joy in the fullness of life which Jesus said he had come to bring.

Jeu d'Esprit

Flame-dancing Spirit, come,
Sweep us off our feet and
Dance us through our days.
Surprise us with your rhythms,
Dare us to try new steps, explore
New patterns and new partnerships.
Release us from old routines
To swing in abandoned joy
And fearful adventure.
And in the intervals,
Rest us,
In your still centre.

Eucharistic Prayer for Pentecost

Eternal God:
We praise you for your glory.

We praise you that in Jesus,
now risen and glorified,
you offer us fullness of life
beyond our imagining:
Raise us to life with him.

We praise you for the Spirit's
disturbing presence, urging us on
to explore the riches of your love:
Open our hearts to your transforming power.

Open us up to your glory, Lord, as
with angels and archangels, and
all who have responded to your call,
we praise you, saying:
Holy, holy, holy Lord,
God of power and joy,
heaven and earth are full of your glory,
all praise to your name.

Be with us now, Lord God,
as we remember Jesus, who
the night before he died,
took bread and wine, blessed them,
and gave them to his friends, saying,
'This is my body given for you.
This is my blood, shed for you.
Eat and drink to remember me.'

Come freshly to us, living God,
as we share these holy gifts.
Flame-dancing Spirit come:
**Sweep us off our feet and
dance us through our days.**

Surprise us with your rhythms:
**Dare us to try new steps, explore
new patterns and new partnerships.**

Release us from old routines:
**To swing in abandoned joy
and fearful adventure.**

And in the intervals:
Rest us in your still centre. Amen.

Section 3

Ordinary Time

Ordinary Time

All the excitement is over for another year in terms of the Church's calendar. For half the year, the calendar gives us a framework within which to pray and live. It starts with Advent, a time of waiting, if we can manage it with all the competing commercial and domestic preparations for Christmas. Then there's the celebration of God coming into the world in human form. We're caught up in the wonder of it all, we hear the angels' song and marvel at the variety of visitors to the newborn child. We watch his parents go through the processes required by the Law when they present him to God in the Temple. Then, after a brief pause, we are plunged into Lent, Holy Week, Good Friday, Easter, the Ascension and Pentecost. There's so much to take in that, though we repeat the cycle every year, we always seem to find new truths to reflect on, new depths to the love of God.

And on the day after Pentecost, the Church's calendar says in small type, 'Ordinary Time resumes today.' There are no major festivals between Pentecost and Advent except for Trinity: God in all God's mystery and wonder. That's all we've got, and all we need. As Julian of Norwich said, 'In God we have all.'

And it's 'Ordinary Time', the name given to the parts of the year when there are no major fasts or feasts to be observed, only God. We hardly noticed the other period of Ordinary Time, a few weeks between the Presentation in the Temple and the beginning of Lent. Now we've got six months, the long green season of Trinity. But it's not six months for doing nothing in particular: green, the liturgical colour for the season, is also the colour we associate with growth. So we've got six months to digest all that

we received in the earlier period of intense attention
to God's activity in Jesus, six months to learn what it
means to live in the power of the Spirit, six months to
wonder at the splendour and mystery of God, six
months of good growing time before we take
ourselves into the new cycle and new discoveries
about God and ourselves.

When you think about it, 'Ordinary Time' is a
strange term, because whatever else time is, it is
hardly 'ordinary'. Time is a great mystery. It does
funny things. Or perhaps it is our attitude to time,
rather than time itself, which is odd. We say that we
have 24 hours in every day, but sometimes we
wonder where time has gone. We run out of it, we
waste it, we kill it, or it hangs heavy for us. We make
time when we want to do something, we buy time
when we're not sure what to do, we mark time when
we're waiting, we save time (but never seem to be
able to find the time we've saved when we want it),
we say we haven't got time when we want to get out of
something.

The ordered division of time into days, hours,
minutes, is what we have developed in order for
society to operate. Musicians know about that: if they
want to play together, one of the first things they have
to learn is to keep time. But people have very
different attitudes to time: some are bound by it,
always punctual, never missing deadlines; others are
much more casual. There are cultural differences of
approach too: our western preoccupation with time is
viewed with amusement or exasperation by people in
other parts of the world – 'You have clocks,' they say,
'we have time.'

Now we have time. Time to let what we have learnt
take root, and come to fruition in our lives. The truth
of the incarnation is that God meets us in time, in the
events and encounters of daily life. The Bible talks

about time in different ways. There is 'chronos', clock time, and there is 'kairos', the judgement time, the time when God breaks into clock time, and we either recognize him or we miss him, rather like the woman and Simon the Pharisee in the encounter recorded in the gospel (Luke 7.36-50). The woman responded to God in Jesus, but Simon dismissed him as not worth the ordinary courtesies of hospitality, almost as though, in spite of having invited him for a meal, he didn't want to give him the time of day.

God is always stepping into our ordinary time, challenging and surprising us into new awareness. We don't have to wait until Advent comes round again to learn to be alert, to keep awake, to remind ourselves to look for the signs of God's coming in the things that we do, the people we meet. We've got time to grow and be nourished by God's gifts: to be strengthened in faith, built up in hope and grow in love; and all for the sake of Jesus Christ, our Lord.

Eucharistic Prayer for daily life

Creator God, in whose design
joy and woe are woven together,
we thank you for calling us
to work with you in weaving
the fabric of your kingdom.

We thank you that
in your Son Jesus Christ,
you have given us a pattern for ministry,
and that yoked with him
in joys and sorrows
we have strength for the task.

Be with us now
as we remember Jesus,
who, on the night before he died,
took bread and wine, blessed them
and gave them to his friends, saying,
'This is my body, given for you.
This is my blood, shed for you.
Eat and drink to remember me.'

Come freshly to us now, Lord God,
and in the midst of struggle keep us
joyful in hope.
Pour out your Holy Spirit as we
bring before you these gifts and
remember Christ's sacrifice
made once for all on the cross.
Feed us with his body and blood
that we may live and grow in him.

Pick up the threads of our experience;
craft your pattern in us and through us,
and in your time reveal its significance;
for you are the God who
weaves the opportunities of our daily lives,
our joys and sorrows,
into the glory of your eternal kingdom. **Amen.**

Trinity Sunday

You have probably heard the story about the church where on Trinity Sunday, as the *Book of Common Prayer* requires, the congregation was reciting the Athanasian Creed, with its rolling statements:

> 'The Father incomprehensible, the Son incomprehensible and the Holy Spirit incomprehensible ...' and a crochety voice from the pews said, 'If you ask me, the whole darned thing is incomprehensible.'

And that's what Trinity Sunday is all about. God *is* incomprehensible, far beyond our understanding, greater by far than our imagining.

We've spent half the Christian year learning about God's dealings with his people. Year by year, we read in Scripture how God created women and men in his own image, to live by his laws. We have heard again how human beings chose to go their own way with the consequent loss of their closeness to God and each other. But God never gave up on them. Over and over again, God called his people with yearning love; and over and over again, people responded and then fell away. And, at last, God spoke in a living word, Jesus, the embodiment of God's love. We have heard his words, and seen his way of life, which go right to the heart of what it means to live in close relationship with God. We watched the struggle with the powers of evil focused on the cross. We saw apparent defeat turned round again by a mighty act of God in the resurrection. We kept company with Christ during the great 40 days as he opened the scriptures to people who had missed the point. We acknowledged the end of his earthly ministry at the ascension, and we waited with eager anticipation for the coming of the Spirit at Pentecost. So our experience has been of God as Father, Son and Holy Spirit: Creator, Redeemer and Sanctifier.

And then comes Trinity Sunday, and we realize that we don't understand, and that perhaps in this life we never will, because there is always more. We cannot define God, because any definition limits God to what our human minds can hold. And always there is more. Jesus said that the Spirit would lead us into truth (John 16.13). Discovering God is a journey.

Those who tried to describe God in Scripture often had difficulty in finding the right words. Think of Ezekiel. In his attempt to describe his vision of God (Ezekiel 1) he couldn't get any closer than repeatedly saying, 'there was something like ...'. And he ended with the words, 'This was the appearance of the likeness of the glory of God.' His response was to fall down in worship. The same response is called out in a very similar vision recorded in Revelation 4. The vision of God calls us to worship. 'You are worthy, our Lord and God, to receive glory and honour and power, for you created all things, and by your will they existed and were created' (Revelation 4.11).

Of course, we must look for ways of expressing our understanding of God, so that we can share our good news. But we must never think that we can define God. Scripture teaches us that the appropriate response to coming closer to God is worship. Worship takes us beyond our definitions, and brings us closer to poetry than to prose.

Trinity Sunday reminds us that God is a God who continually surprises us into fresh understanding. And yet there is more.

Eucharistic Prayer for Trinity
(*with Peruvian Gloria*)

Blessed are you, Lord God,
that you are always and only God:
Blessed are you, Lord God.

Blessed are you, Lord God,
that you have revealed yourself
in Jesus Christ:
Blessed are you, Lord God.

Blessed are you, Lord God,
for you lead us to know you
through your Spirit:
Blessed are you, Lord God.

Holy God, vulnerable and strong,
we praise and bless you,
and with all who adore you
in earth and heaven, we sing:

Glory to God, Glory to God, Glory to the Father
**Glory to God, Glory to God, Glory to the
    Father**
To God be glory for ever
To God be glory for ever
Alleluia, Amen. **Alleluia, Amen; Alleluia, Amen.**

Glory to God, Glory to God, Glory to Christ Jesus
(*Repeat as above*)

Glory to God, Glory to God, Glory to the Spirit
(*Repeat as above*)

All praise and glory be to you, Lord God,
as we remember Jesus, who
the night before he died,
took bread and wine, blessed them
and gave them to his friends, saying,
'This is my body, this is my blood.
Eat and drink to remember me.'

Come freshly to us now, Lord God,
and fill us with your grace.

**May our hearts overflow with love for you,
our spirits dance with joy in you,
our wills be drawn by desire for you;
for you have called us
to be your friends, and live
to your praise and glory. Amen.**

Leading a balanced life –
The advantage of having a Rule

The idea of a Rule of Life does not sit easily in the vocabulary of many people today. But we probably all have one. There are things we do as a rule which keep us healthy: we eat, drink and wash. We work (taking that in its broadest sense, not just the gainful employment aspect) and we know that for the sake of our health and sanity we need recreation and holidays, and an appropriate amount of sleep. So, as a rule, we have meals at regular times, we go to bed at a similar time most days, and get up at a similar time most mornings. This rule does not imprison us – if we need to be up very early one day, we might go to bed a bit earlier the night before. If we have a late night, we sleep in the next day. If we're camping in the wilds perhaps we don't wash as often as when we have water on tap. Our pattern of life can be flexible, but we are mostly glad of a routine which sustains us. The decisions we make about the routine mean that we don't have to waste energy deciding every day about things which we know are necessary to our health.

The same principle applies in our spiritual life too. We know that for our spiritual health there are things we need to do and the language is important. We perhaps began doing things because we were told we *ought* to, but until we recognize the *need* we don't take them on for ourselves. We had to learn, when we were little, about eating sensibly, about washing regularly (especially the bits we didn't think anyone could see), about adequate rest. As we grew up these things became natural, even desirable. I often think, as I hear a child protesting about bedtime, that it won't be long before, like many adults, that child will be thankful to be able to go to bed!

We seem to take a little longer to get to spiritual maturity. We need a reminder to help us to live a balanced life. And that's where a Rule of Life comes in. We decide what the essential elements of life are, and how we are going to give them proper attention. Making a decision about personal prayer, joining in public worship, a simple lifestyle, use of money, recreation, proper time with family and friends, saves us having to reinvent our plan every day, helps us to prioritize what we need, and ensures that we don't leave important elements of our inner life to chance.

Benedict, who lived in the sixth century, was responsible for the Rule which became the foundation of monastic life in its various forms. Prayer was at the centre of his Rule: the monks and nuns met seven times a day for corporate worship. The rest of the time was divided between work, study and rest. His Rule provided for an ordered and balanced life, where all people from the apparently most important to the seemingly unimportant were to be treated with respect; where food and drink were to be provided so that no one was in want; where all tools and clothing were to be looked after, and all in the context of learning to find God in all things. 'Prefer nothing to the love of Christ' is the requirement at the heart of the Rule. But it is not a straitjacket, it's a guide.

A Rule of Life helps us to keep our balance amid all the demands made on us. It reminds us that prayer is the foundation of the whole of our life, it is our relationship with God in action. So our commitment to God is worked out in the way we live, how we love our neighbour and how we love ourselves. Paying attention to our need for rest and recreation will make us more available to others, and including in our care for others concern for the resources of the created world will ensure that we reflect God's delight in all that is.

Benedict encouraged discipline, but he required it to be practised with a certain lightness of touch. Monks were enjoined quietly (for this was during Greater Silence) to encourage one another as they arose for the Night Office, 'for the sleepy like to make excuses' (Ch. 22 of the *Rule*). All were expected to be in their places in chapel at the latest by the end of the opening Psalm, but Benedict ordered that the first Psalm at Lauds, the early morning Office, should always be said slowly, so that everyone stood a chance of getting there (Ch. 13 of the *Rule*).

What we do 'as a rule' must not be a burden, but a framework which frees us to grow in love. Rooted in paying attention to God, like the Celts who had a prayer for every occasion, we learn to make the connections, and live every part of our lives to God's praise and glory.

Eucharistic Prayer – St Benedict

Lord God, we praise you
for your servant Benedict,
who turned from earthly wealth
to discover the rich simplicity
of your love:
**Lord, teach us to measure our lives
by the fullness of Christ.**

We thank you for Benedict's insight
that all relationships should be
governed by humility:
**Teach us to respect each other
and all creation.**

We thank you for his teaching
that obedience is the
touchstone of faith:
**Lord, bring our hearts back
to desire your will.**

We thank you for his insistence
that where we are
is where we shall find you:
Lord, open our eyes that we may see.

With Benedict and all whose lives
have been inspired by his Rule,
we join angels and archangels
and the whole company of heaven, saying:
**Holy, holy, holy Lord,
God of life and love,
heaven and earth are full of your glory,
all praise to your name.**

Be with us, Lord God,
as we remember Jesus,
who on the night before he died,
took bread and wine, gave you thanks,
and gave them to his friends, saying,
'This is my body, this is my blood.
Eat and drink to remember me.'

**Come to us now, Lord God,
and call us afresh to your service.
Keep us faithful, make us joyful,
for you are the God who delights in us
and rejoices to call us your friends. Amen.**

Quiet Day

What is a Quiet Day for? Most of us rush around from one thing to another for much of the time. A Quiet Day offers us space to rest and recover ourselves. Quite often, if we do nothing we suffer from a terrible feeling of guilt, because we've inherited the view that really we ought always to be on the go. Not all the Victorian values were good ones, and the reinforcement of Kipling's idea about 'filling the unforgiving minute with sixty seconds' worth of distance run' (in his poem 'If'), which hymns like 'Father, hear the prayer we offer' put in front of us, encourages a kind of spirituality which leaves no time for resting in God.

My response to that hymn is the poem

The prayer we offer

Not for ease? Why not?
What's wrong with ease?
For most of us the
Problem is not self-indulgence,
But that we allow ourselves too little.
Prohibitions, counsels of perfection,
Drive us and load us up with guilt.

Time enough for courageous living
And all that rock-smiting.
Let's rest and wander in green pastures
When we find them, make the space
To let ourselves be loved;
Build up our strength
And grow in confidence;
Drink living water springing in
Great fountains;
Feed on the Bread of Life which
Satisfies.

Then we shall have provision
For the journey, and at last
Arrive, not too unpractised
In the art of resting
In his presence.

A Quiet Day gives us just that opportunity for letting ourselves be loved. We don't *have* to do anything – it's not a day for catching up on odd jobs or unwritten letters, or even reading a good book. It's a day for doing nothing with God, letting God slow us down, fill us with his life, and send us back to what we call 'normal' life with fresh courage and a deeper sense of God's presence. If you haven't got time, it's definitely a day for you.

Planning and leading a Quiet Day

The leader and the organizer of a Quiet Day need to be in touch well in advance, to discuss the form and content of the day, so that the event itself can run smoothly.

Also think about the cost of the day. How much will the venue charge? What expenses will the leader incur? Does the leader expect a fee? It is a good idea to give the leader a token of some kind if there is no fee involved – a lot of work goes into the preparation, and participants should have the opportunity to recognize that.

With regard to the content of the day, consider who the day is for. Will participants be familiar with the use of silence, or new to it? For some, the idea of a day spent in silence sounds very attractive, for others it's rather daunting. For people who live alone, and perhaps meet few people in the course of daily life, to spend time with others but not be able to talk to them might be very hard, even cruel. There are no brownie points awarded for the length of time we spend in silence, but stillness does deepen if we give it a chance, so arrange for definite periods of quiet during the day. The crunch point usually comes at lunch time. Perhaps it would be possible to set aside one area for people who want to be quiet all day, and then people could choose whether to talk or not as they eat. (It is probably a good idea for the leader to join any non-silent group at lunch, so that they don't feel in any way 'second class'.) Usually the simplest way to provide lunch is for people to bring their own. If lunch is being provided, and will be served in one place, negotiate with the group at the beginning of the day, or beforehand, about the place of silence during the day. Whatever the experience of participants, or lack of it, some basic help at the beginning of the day about using the time will be welcomed.

It might be helpful to call the event 'A Day for Quiet Reflection', rather than 'A Quiet Day'. Make it clear in the publicity material what is likely to happen, so that people know what to expect. A basic programme might look like this:

10.00	Arrive, coffee
10.15	Worship, introduction of theme and first address followed by time for personal reflection
12 noon	Corporate prayer or a simple Eucharist
12.30	Lunch
1.30	Address followed by time for personal reflection
2.45	Closing worship
3.00	Tea and depart.

The times can be adjusted, but some people will have children to collect from school, or other commitments in the early evening, so it is best not to end too late.

The content of the day may be requested by the group, or it may be left to the leader to decide. Whatever it is, the leader needs to be clear in his/her own mind about the content of the day. The participants should be given clear indications about timing, and offered a variety of activities (without compulsion!) for the periods of personal reflection. The most important activity is to do nothing, and let God love us, but most of us need a few ideas to explore to help us reach that kind of stillness.

Choose the venue with care, and if possible visit it before you decide to use it. It should be warm (well ventilated in summer) and reasonably comfortable to sit in, with a kitchen so that people can make drinks when they want them, and loos nearby. You do not have to go into the depths of the country – in fact, it's bad theology to think that we can't be still and meet God in the middle of a city. But the content of the day will to some extent be determined by the environment, and perhaps by the weather.

Wherever the day is held, if possible find a space where the corporate parts of the day can be contained, such as a chapel or a circle of chairs. Provide a worship focus – candle, icon, flowers, and perhaps a helpful background aroma. Make sure you can be heard – use a loop system if it exists.

Checklist for the organizer

Do participants know what they need to bring, such as a Bible, and material to write or draw with?

Do they know what the day will cost?

Are people sure about travel arrangements?

Will there be a Eucharist? What will be needed for it?

Checklist for the leader

Do you have everything that you need: copies of any material you want people to ponder over, Bible references; words of hymns/songs; candles?

If you want to sing, can you lead the singing unaccompanied? If you need accompaniment, do you know if anyone can play the flute/violin/guitar? (More suitable for a small group than piano/organ.)

Will you need a tape recorder/CD player? (Don't forget to bring CDs/tapes.) Is there a convenient socket to plug a machine into, or will you need an extension lead?

If there is to be a Eucharist, what do you need to provide?

Remember, people have come to spend time with God. The leader's job is to enable that, not to fill the space. **Be brief.**

Give basic guidance as the day progresses. **Be simple.**

What leaders have to offer springs out of their own prayerfulness. **Be prepared through prayer, and make sure that there is a network of people praying for the day.**

A simple order for a Eucharist

The principle behind this order of service is that there should be few words, and plenty of space for reflection. The whole order is intended to reflect confidence in the love of God who has put away our sin, and welcomes us as his chosen people. Familiar prayers can be used, but sparingly. It is possible to use this outline for an extended Eucharist on the last morning of a retreat, with the last address forming part of the Ministry of the Word, and a break for reflection (and possibly coffee) preceding the Offertory.

Preparation (a simple prayer invoking the Holy Spirit)

Invitation to confession (based on words from Julian of Norwich)

The Lord looks on his servants with pity,
not with blame.
In our sight we do not stand;
in God's sight we do not fall.
Both these insights are true,
but the greater belongs to God.

Confession

Either leave space for silent confession, or use the following form:

Lord God, you have made us for yourself, and long for our love;
forgive our reluctance to respond to you.
Lord, have mercy:
Lord, have mercy.

Lord Christ, you bring us healing and forgiveness;
forgive our unwillingness to accept your gifts.
Christ, have mercy:
Christ, have mercy.

Lord Spirit, you come to us with new life;
forgive our desire to cling on to old ways.
Lord, have mercy:
Lord, have mercy.

Absolution

Our merciful God has put away your (our) sin.
Let us take hold of this forgiveness, and live
in confidence and peace. **Amen.**

Collect

Reading(s)

Silence for reflection

Prayers – the litany for the world, at the end of the
section on Praying for the world, section 1 p. 33,
would be a useful, simple form of intercession.

Offertory – as well as the traditional prayers at the
offering of the bread and wine, it would be
appropriate to say:
Blessed are you, Lord God of all creation,
of your goodness we have *our* gifts to offer.
Blessed by your grace, we shall shine as lights in the
world.

Eucharistic Prayer

(There are several Eucharistic prayers with the
seasonal material in this book.)

The Lord's Prayer

Invitation to share Communion

(It would be good at this point, if not before, if participants were in a circle, so that they could give the bread and wine to each other. If words are required, the *Wee Worship Book*, Fourth Incarnation, from the Iona Community has some suggestions.)

Share Communion

Prayer of thanksgiving

Blessing and Dismissal (Jeu D'Esprit)

Flame-dancing Spirit, come,
Sweep us off our feet and
Dance us through our days.
Surprise us with your rhythms,
Dare us to try new steps, explore
New patterns and new partnerships.
Release us from old routines
To swing in abandoned joy
And fearful adventure.
And in the intervals,
Rest us,
In your still centre.

We go in peace to love and serve the Lord:
In the name of Christ. Amen.

A day to let God love you

Material for a Quiet Day using the pattern set out in 'Planning and leading a Quiet Day' (section 3 p. 153).

Preparation

It will be helpful to have:

A handout listing Bible references: Genesis 1.26, 31; Isaiah 43.4; Ephesians 2.8-10 (Jerusalem Bible version); Mark 10.17-22 (rich young man); Luke 19.1-10 (Zacchaeus); Matthew 16.13-23, 26.31-46, Luke 22.54-62, John 21.15-17 (Peter); John 15.12-17, and the poem 'Revelation'. This can be given to participants after the first session to help them follow up the material if they want to – there won't be an examination at the end of the day!

Another handout for the afternoon session, containing the extract from Henri Nouwen's *Life of the Beloved*. (Found in the section 'Becoming the Beloved – Taken'.)

A reproduction of Michelangelo's *Captives* is a useful visual aid.

A candle as a centre focus. Individual candles for use in closing worship.

Material for worship, including a map of the world and leaves.

Outline for introductory address

Today you haven't got to do anything but let God love you. We're not very good at doing that. We put a lot of energy into working out how we can love God, but we don't let God have much of a chance to love us. That is partly because we don't think we are very lovable. If God knew what I was really like, he'd never love me – but when we catch ourselves thinking like that, it's time to reassess things.

St Theresa told her nuns to try thinking of God looking at them lovingly and humbly. That's not the way we often think about God looking at us. We carry within us still folk memories of the Victorian all-seeing eye of God, looking at everything we do, and disapproving of most of it.

But that is not the biblical view of God and God's relationship with us. First of all, we are told that we are made in the image of God, (Genesis 1.26) and that when he had made everything, he was delighted with it (Genesis 1.31). Then Paul tells us (in Ephesians 2.10 in the Jerusalem Bible version) that we are God's work of art. Not the description we often give ourselves, perhaps. But if we have ever looked at anything we have made and thought that it's pretty good, then we begin to understand something of what God feels for each one of us. We are precious and honoured, and loved (Isaiah 43.4).

That doesn't mean that we are perfect. We have some way to go still – we are a bit like Michelangelo's *Captives*, still in the process of being completed. But not being complete is the human condition. Even when our flaws are to be laid at our own door, what in church language we call 'sin' is not the most important thing about us. The most important thing is what God sees – our potential, our giftedness, the special qualities each one of us has. It would be wonderful if, each time we met for worship, we could balance the time we spend reflecting on our sinfulness by spending some time reflecting thankfully on our giftedness. That would help us to get our view of ourselves back into God's perspective. We might also be able to think of him more realistically as our Father: most parents talking about their children rejoice in their good points, rather than dwelling on their bad ones. And even when talking about their naughtiness, they find it difficult sometimes to keep their faces straight. I wonder sometimes whether God has the same difficulty with us!

We can learn about the way God looks at us by thinking about the way Jesus looked at people in his encounters.

He looked at the rich young man with love, as he told him to get rid of his riches and then follow him. The young man couldn't do it. But I wonder if, when he reflected on the conversation later, he realized that for the first time someone had told him to give his wealth away because he was wanted for himself, not for what he had got? Did he, perhaps, in the end, decide to follow?

Jesus looked up to Zacchaeus, and told him he wanted to spend time with him. The first time for years, perhaps, that anyone had looked *up* to Zacchaeus, and seen him for who he really was. We know the transformation that resulted from that look.

And Peter – Jesus looked at him in the courtyard, just after Peter had denied knowing him. It must have been a look of love and acceptance to make Peter weep bitterly. And then, after the resurrection, by another charcoal fire, Jesus restored Peter through his threefold question, 'Do you love me?' The language in the Greek is significant. When Jesus asked the question, Peter responded with a rather weaker word for love, 'I am your friend.' The second time the same thing happens. But the third time, Jesus uses Peter's word, 'Are you my friend?' Peter is uncomfortable at the questioning – but Jesus doesn't go on to say that when Peter can love him properly, he will entrust him with his work; he commissions him there and then, and helps Peter move towards wholeness again.

That is most encouraging for us in our discipleship – whatever the level of commitment we can give, Jesus looks at us with love, and takes us as we are, so that he can grow us to wholeness.

So this morning, think about God looking at you with love, appreciating you and your gifts, and rejoice with God in them.

Go on, Lord,
Love me into wholeness,
Set me free
To share with you
In your creative joy;
To laugh with you
At your delight
In me,
Your work of art.

('Revelation')

Midday prayer (or Simple Eucharist)

Use the map and leaves as suggested in 'Praying for the world' (in Section 1 p. 32). Being loved by God, and special to him, is not the same as being spoilt, so it is good to spend time praying for all whom God loves, and for whom we feel concern.

Outline for second address

'You are precious in my eyes and honoured, and I love you' (Isaiah 43.4).

What, me? We are so conditioned to backing off from compliments and thanks that we find it very difficult to accept that we are loved. Just think of how we respond when someone gives us an unexpected present. 'Oh, you shouldn't have done that,' we say.

Or 'You shouldn't have spent all that on me'! What does that say about our sense of self-worth?

Jesus says we are special. We have been chosen. But we have had so many experiences of not being chosen that it is hard to believe. It all began probably in the playground when the teams were being picked, and the best friends and the good at games got chosen first. The group of those not picked got smaller and smaller, and there was an awful feeling that I might be the only one left, not really wanted but having to join the team because you had to go somewhere. We can all remember hurts like that. And there may well have been more serious ones, when relationships didn't work out, or a coveted job went to someone else. It's easy to think we're not worth much.

But Jesus says he has chosen us. We often get our discipleship the wrong way round, and think we have chosen him. But his love always draws us before we respond. And his choice is that we become his friends, working with him, bearing fruit as his life flows through us. Henri Nouwen, in *Life of the Beloved* says, 'The great spiritual battle begins – and never ends – with the reclaiming of our chosen-ness.' We have to allow God to look at us and say, 'You are precious, I have chosen you, and love you', and not draw back.

We can all think of reasons why we can't be special and chosen. But we have to challenge those thoughts whenever they come up within us, or attack us from outside, and assert again that we have been chosen by God for himself. But we are not more special than God's other people. When we really begin to learn about love, we learn that the more we give away, the more we have. Becoming confident in our own sense of being loved will enable us to help others to be aware that they are loved too.

And perhaps we shall be able to challenge the heresy that we always have to be on the go to earn God's favour. Let's look at our diaries, and see whether we could plan to have time to let God love us every day.

That's something we could try to do this afternoon, as we think about the fact that we have been chosen, and ask for grace to let that truth sink deep into our hearts.

Closing worship

Spend time in thanksgiving for the day.

Give participants the opportunity to light an individual candle as an act of commitment to live as people chosen and loved. These can be placed on the map, since it is in the world that we live out our calling.

Encourage people to take a candle with them as they leave. The quiet day will be over, but what has begun in it will continue as life goes on.

A day with Julian of Norwich
Material for a Quiet Day

This material uses some of the ideas set out in 'A day to let God love you', but takes the illustrations from *The Revelation of Divine Love* by Julian of Norwich.

Preparation

It will be helpful to have:

Handouts containing extracts from chapters 4,46,48, 52, 58,59,62 of the Long Text of the *Revelation of Divine Love*, and Bible references for maternal imagery for God: Deuteronomy 32.11-12, 18; 33.27; Isaiah 49.15; Hosea 11.1-4; Matthew 23.37, together with Anselm's Canticle beginning 'Jesus, as a mother you gather your people to you,' for follow-up to the first session, and from chapters 39, 40, 73 and 82 of the Long Text for the second session.

For midday worship, use the map of the world and hazelnuts.

At closing worship, individual candles.

Outline for first address

'Everything has being through the love of God.' 'All will be well.'

Julian's message was nothing like the facile message given by some Christians: 'God's in his heaven, all's right with the world.'

Julian knew from her experience that all was not right with the world. Give a brief summary of the current situation in Church and state during her lifetime: The Hundred Years' War began and continued; there were outbreaks of plague; political unrest leading to the Peasants' Revolt; cattle plague and poor harvests.

Julian's conviction that all will be well came out of her experience when she was just over 30, when she was seriously ill, and was granted a series of visions of Christ, accompanied by revelations of the depth of God's love. From them she drew understanding of the nature of God, and the nature of humanity.

First of all, God.

What is your preferred imagery for God? By what name do you address God? We have got very used to particular ways of addressing or describing God. 'Father' is the most usual and, in hymns, 'King', 'Judge' and 'Shepherd' probably come next in popularity. But we've got stuck, probably because we take Jesus seriously when he said, 'When you pray, say "Our Father".' But when he said that, I wonder whether he wasn't simply suggesting another idea to play with – Father is not a prominent image in the Jewish scriptures.

There is much maternal imagery in Scripture, and when Julian suggested that we might think of God as Mother, she was not the first theologian to do so. Anselm of Canterbury in the tenth century had done so too. Julian attributes to our Mother God our creation, our care in mercy and pity, our sustenance not with milk but with the precious food of true life in the Sacrament. Just as a mother does not want her children to suffer, even to the point of giving her life for them, so God in Jesus our Mother brings us by his death to eternal life.

It isn't necessarily more helpful to address God as Mother than it is to address God as Father – both titles can raise difficulties for people because of their own experiences. But it does widen our understanding to consider the imagery we use. Part of our difficulty lies in the way the English language attaches gender to nouns and pronouns – in many languages that isn't the case, and God has to be God. It is worth noting that imagery is a gift to play with, not a strait-jacket to pin God down. We don't turn God into anything by the imagery we use – God doesn't become a rock just because the Psalmist described God in that way. But we are perhaps in danger of turning our idea of God into an idol if we are unwilling to countenance fresh imagery.

So this morning, ponder on imagery. Experiment a little with ideas that may be fresh to you, but are actually very old. You might like to look at the biblical passages referred to. But all our thinking needs to send us back to God, for as Julian said, 'Only in God we have all.'

Midday prayer (or simple Eucharist)

Use map and hazelnuts. (See Praying for the world, Section 1 p. 32.)

Outline for second address

Where does what we were thinking about this morning leave us? How does our imagery for God help us to understand ourselves, and our relationship with God? The way people talk, you would think that God is out to get us. Insurance companies describe as acts of God anything they regard as too nasty to be recognized as qualifying for compensation, never anything good! And we persist in asking what we have done to deserve the things which happen to us, as though God sends suffering and hardship to punish us, even when we don't deserve it. What loving father/mother would act like that?

We have to recognize the fact of sin. But Julian had some very liberating things to say about sin. It is nothing, not because it doesn't exist – it is the sharpest scourge that can afflict us. It is nothing, because it has no status; God has dealt with it, and sin is forgiven. For Julian, feelings of guilt and worthlessness are far more damaging than the failures we call sin, because they fix our attention on ourselves. What really delights God is our delight in him, and preoccupation with sin distracts us from that.

'Our courteous Lord does not want his servants to despair because they fall often and grievously, for our falling does not hinder him in loving us. In our sight we do not stand, in God's sight we do not fall.' Both these insights are true, but the greater belongs to God.

To God, we are infinitely precious and loved, and grasping that truth will help us build up our confidence, and sense of self-worth. For we are chosen. We can all think of reasons why we are not worth choosing, but those are lies. The truth is that we are chosen by God, and God wants us to value ourselves. That doesn't mean that we don't need to change – confession and forgiveness are still necessary. But forgiveness sets us free to move on and grow in confidence in God's love.

There will be several outcomes to this sense of growing self-worth. We will have the grace to stop putting ourselves down by describing ourselves as unworthy recipients of God's love. We might be able to accept gifts and compliments without responding with 'Oh, you shouldn't have done that!' We shall learn that what is true of us is true of everyone else too, and that will affect the way we treat others, and the range of our prayerful support. We shall grow in understanding that we are chosen not so that we can feel smug about it, but because we are meant to bear fruit. That entails pruning, having the dead wood in our lives cut out, letting God train us in the way we need to grow.

We are God's work of art – not finished, but on-the-way people. So this afternoon, ponder on your chosen-ness, and think about how life could be different if we really dared to believe that we are precious to God.

Closing worship

Spend time in thanksgiving for the day.

Give participants the opportunity to light an individual candle as an act of commitment to live as people chosen and loved. These can be placed on the map, since it is in the world that we live out our calling.

Encourage people to take a candle with them as they leave. The Quiet Day will be over, but what has begun in it will continue as life goes on.

Eucharistic Prayer – Julian of Norwich

Lord God,
through your servant Julian
you revealed to us that
as Father you are all power and goodness,
and as Mother you are all wisdom and love:
We praise and glorify you.

We praise you that you hold
all creation in your love,
and enfold all creatures in your care:
We praise and glorify you.

With angels and archangels
and the whole company of heaven
we sing:
Holy, holy, holy Lord,
God of life and love,
Heaven and earth are full of your glory,
all praise to your name.

Come to us now, Lord God,
as we remember Jesus, who,
on the night before he died,
took bread and wine, blessed them
and gave them to his friends, saying,
'This is my body, this is my blood.
Eat and drink to remember me.'

Come to us now, most courteous God,
and fill our hearts with longing for you:
God of your goodness, give us yourself.

Take from us all hesitancy and fear:
God of your goodness, give us yourself.

Draw us to delight in you, for you are
the God who longs for our love:
God of your goodness, give us yourself,
for we can ask for nothing less
than that which can do you full worship.
If we ask anything less,
we shall always be in want.
Only in you we have all. Amen.

A day for carers

A day for carers provides much-needed respite for people who often have little time for themselves, and the programme needs above all to provide space, without much formal input from the leader, who for this purpose could well be renamed the host. Carers often get so overwhelmed by the demands of care that they push their own needs aside, and it is good to offer people a little pampering when they do find time to get away. It is important to have a venue which is comfortable.

I have been blessed in being able to use a local retreat house where we hold two such days most years. Old Alresford Place, in Hampshire, is set in lovely grounds. In the winter we can have a log fire in the sitting-room, and those who come always appreciate the way the table is laid for lunch, and the care with which the food is presented. I have found it helpful to work, on alternate days, alongside an aromatherapist who offers hand massage, and a podiatrist who offers foot massage. We have a general rule that, for the morning at least, we don't talk to the other carers about what we do, so that everyone has a chance to get away from the demands. This is not a day for the exchange of information – other bodies provide days of that kind. While the aroma-therapist/podiatrist are plying their skill, I make myself available for personal conversation with anyone who wants to come. I was a carer for nine years myself as my mother became increasingly infirm and senile, and for the last 15 months of her life she was in a home, so I understand something of what people are going through. At lunch we talk, and in the afternoon people either go on with their own pursuits, or enjoy each other's company on a walk, or sitting in the garden or by the fire.

A pattern for the day

Provide coffee as people arrive

(It may not be possible for everyone to arrive for the formal beginning, so make sure there is always someone on hand to make people feel welcome when they do arrive.) If possible, make sure that people can make drinks as and when they want to.

Gathering to set the scene

Light a candle as a reminder for us that Jesus, the light of the world, is with us, and that we are being prayed for.

Play some music to help people 'arrive' and begin to unwind.

Introductory talk

You are special not because you are carers, but because you are the people you are, and God loves you (Isaiah 43.4). We don't always feel that we are special – people tell us sometimes that we are wonderful because of what we do, but we know that caring sometimes brings out the worst in us, and we can feel very guilty about the resentment and irritation that can make us less than kind or even positively murderous. Sometimes we feel guilt about the decisions we have to make about involving professional care in a home. I was greatly helped in this by a comment made to a friend of mine about the situation she was in, long before it became an issue for me. She was told, 'Your mother needs two things, love and care. At the moment, the demands made on you by her care are so great that it is difficult for you to love her. If you can arrange for your mother to be cared for, you will be free to love her.' We don't have to beat ourselves up about having negative feelings – but we need to develop some strategies for making sure that those we care for don't get the rough end of our temper. Time away, like today, is one way of restoring our balance.

Today, you haven't got to do anything. It's time for you. As a physical reminder that you have left your duties behind, write your name on the card, and the name of the person/situation you are having time away from, and put in the bowl/on the altar, next to the candle which reminds us that we are all in God's hands. We can safely leave our care to him and the people who are standing in for us today. At the end of the day, you can pick the card up again, as you pick up your duties.

I'm going to suggest that we give each other space to get away from the demands – so let's agree that we won't talk to each other about what we have to do as carers, at least for this morning. If you want to talk about your situation, I'm here for you – I know from personal experience what it's like. There is a sheet of paper where you can book your time for personal pampering with hand/foot massage, and you can book a slot with me too if you want. But you don't *have* to do anything! You can walk, sleep, have a long undisturbed bath ... take your time.

During the day

Sometimes I suggest that we have a time of prayer together before lunch.

Sometimes we have a formal ending, largely a time of thanksgiving, and prayer for encouragement as we continue the care.

People are not always able to stay for the whole day, so the host needs to be around as much as possible to make them feel at home while they are there.

Material for use in a Quiet Garden

People who open their gardens for The Quiet Garden Movement sometimes like to offer a theme for the day. These days do not usually have a formal programme following the introductory meditation. If there is a Eucharist, the prayer which follows these suggested themes might be considered to be appropriate.

Theme 1: Consider the flowers

> The kiss of the sun for pardon
> The song of the birds for mirth
> One is nearer God's heart in a garden
> Than anywhere else on earth.

('God's Garden', Dorothy Frances Gurney)

That isn't true, and it's bad theology. What is true is that we often *feel* closer to God. There is peace and refreshment in being alongside the growing life of a garden or the countryside, which often contrasts with the busyness of ordinary life. But that is a city-dweller's view – country people know that there is a lot of hard work behind the tranquillity. And, actually, any gardener knows that there is conflict and a struggle to survive within all growth. And there are always the slugs – a great theological challenge to town- and country-dwellers alike.

But what might we learn from the flowers as we consider them today?

First, each has its own beauty. Take a long look at the flowers, and appreciate their variety in colour and shape, the texture and shade of their greenery.

They all contribute something to the beauty of the whole, partly by enhancing the beauty of other plants.

Don't ignore the plants that don't seem to be doing very much. Some contribute their sober foliage as a background against which others stand out. There are some exotic beauties which seem to stand out on their own, but even they are often glad of a bit of support, especially when the wind and the rain batter them about.

We might go on to think about ourselves. What are our strengths and beauty? What do we contribute to the human herbaceous border which is so dear to God's heart? Some of our gifts may not seem too obvious: like some plants we might look rather dull, or be rather prickly. But it is just those which provide support for the plants around them. So let's acknowledge our nature, and give thanks for who we are, and ask God's blessing on our flowering.

Then we might ponder on the life of plants, and remember that there is always change and growth. If a seed doesn't break open, there will be no plant. If the plant does not flower there will be no chance for it to bear its fruit, which contains the seed for the next generation. The end of all growth is fruitfulness.

In my garden, the prickly firethorn which keeps me at arm's length is covered with berries which will feed the birds, and there is a profusion of love-in-the-mist seed heads which are more beautiful than the flowers. So we might think about ourselves, about our own progress towards fruitfulness. That won't mean for all of us ensuring that there is a new generation to keep the human race going. Our fruitfulness may be in the wisdom we can bring in maturity to our dealings with others, and the way we order our own lives.

And we might remember again how important it is to move on – clinging to the stage where we feel most beautiful or useful, or regretting its passing, means that we prevent ourselves from recognizing the beauty of the present. Some people, like some plants, really come into their own in old age.

The rhythm of nature is sustained by God's love. Our world *is*, our life *is*, because God loves us and wants to bring us to fruitfulness and maturity. And death is part of that process – we carry the seed of eternity within us, which in God's time will be set free.

Theme 2: Trees

The Jewish/Christian story begins in a garden where there were plenty of trees. Only two of them are named: the tree of knowledge, and the tree of life (Genesis 2.9).

We have spent so much of our time in Christian history weighed down by guilt at having tasted the fruit of the forbidden tree, that we seem to have forgotten that God didn't tell anyone not to eat fruit from the tree of life.

Today gives us the opportunity to spend time thinking about that tree, and our lives, as we enjoy the presence of trees in this garden.

One of the images of fulfilment in the Old Testament is a tree. Planted by the waterside, or rooted in worship, trees flourish and bear fruit (Psalm 1.1-3; Jeremiah 17.7-8; Psalm 92.12-15). Jesus used tree imagery too, when he said, 'I am the vine, you are the branches' (John 15.5). Notice that he didn't say, 'I am the *stem*, you are the branches', but 'I am the *vine*'. He enfolds us in his life: we draw his life into ourselves in order to bear fruit. We are inextricably part of him, and he of us. As Paul wrote in Galatians 2.20, 'It is no longer I who live, but it is Christ who lives in me.' Paul used tree imagery also when he wrote in his letter to the Ephesians that it was his prayer for them 'that Christ may dwell in your hearts through faith, as you are being rooted and grounded in love' (Ephesians 3.17). Right at the end of the Bible, the tree of life appears again, and its leaves are for the healing of the nations (Revelation 22.2).

We bring all that to our enjoyment of trees today. And we can add some observations of our own too.

Trees are welcoming – they give life and shelter to myriads of creatures. We enjoy their shelter and shade, and use them as meeting places, trysting places.

They provide stability – we see what happens when rain forests are destroyed, and whole ecological systems are wiped out.

They offer us, as all plants do, a pattern of life that includes death. They can't cling on to any stage of their development: flowers and fruit have to die before new life can be released.

Their roots are amazing: they push through all kinds of debris and unyielding materials in search of life.

So we have plenty of food for thought as we enjoy the trees around us. Let's look and touch, enjoy the texture of the bark, think about the roots, stretch up with the branches. And then let's use our imagination about our own lives. Where are our roots? Can we claim the negative, unyielding bits of our own experience and draw nourishment from them as well as from the more pleasurable springs of life?

And our branches. Do we need to prune our lifestyle so that energy is used more efficiently and fruitfully? Are we welcoming, offering healing in relationships and chance encounters?

But most of all, let's relax into the quiet rhythm of the trees' lives, and feel the sap rising in us again.

Peace Trees

To be in the presence of trees
Is to know peace.
The silent rhythm of their life,
Bringing maturity in due time,
Without anxiety or haste,
Calms our impatience;
Their solid strength, derived from
Hidden roots spreading much further
Than we ever know, gives us security;
Grace, beauty, shapeliness and form,
Delight our senses, soothe our
Fragile nerves, and bring refreshment.

Let us in turn be trees,
Growing in God's time to maturity,
Spreading our roots deep into springs of life,
Opening branches wide to all who come,
Offering strength and healing through our
Peace.

Theme 3: Consider the birds

(This section takes its name from the title of the poem.)

That's one command
I have no problem with.

I held a swallow once,
Knocked senseless by some accident;
Fragile body, tiny beating heart
Cupped in my hand. Then, restored,
With flirt of feathers
Off to freedom flight.

I who have scarcely
Stirred beyond these shores,
Held one who, twice at least,
Had flown four thousand miles.
No map, no compass,
Only unerring inner certainty
Carrying him over land and ocean.
A moment to treasure.

Then there are sparrows,
So common we don't notice them;
Eight a penny, or perhaps ten
Since decimalisation.
I wonder why you didn't tell Job
To look at sparrows, instead of
Parading the juggernauts of your
Creation. After all,
Anyone could make a hippopotamus –
No finesse there, a lump with
Four legs and a great big head –
A child's production.
But a sparrow, there's craftsmanship:
Those shades of brown and gold,
Arranged and sculpted into
Subtly beautiful plumage,
Each one different;
The stocky bodies full of energy,
Brisk, going about their business,
Fighting, squabbling,
Caring for their young, chirping
In incessant cheerfulness.

In contrast to the heron,
Standing more still than a
Contemplative, alert
Waiting for the moment.

And no-one could watch ducks,
Or, better still, listen to them,
Without believing in your sense of humour.

Kingfisher's glory, blackbird's song,
The miracle of flight itself ...
The list is endless.

And we more precious.
A mystery to ponder.

For years now I've been a birdwatcher. Not a twitcher – twitchers rush off whenever something rare or unusual is reported, so that they can say they've seen it, and tick it off on their list. But they don't necessarily learn much about the bird in question, which is often out of context, away from its normal habitat, blown off-course by a storm.

Watchers, on the other hand, wait, look, consider, take time to be where the birds are: a much more contemplative way. They go out in all weathers, sometimes see very little, and from time to time, have one of those rewarding moments which make it all worthwhile.

All that has its parallels in our spiritual life. We sometimes rush off to get the latest spiritual experience, an instant glow of holiness, or a spiritual high. We could learn from the bird *watchers* to be still, alert, but not anxious, eyes open and aware. Ready to receive what we are given.

Bird watching has taught me that all is gift. I may go out hoping to see a particular bird – but it may not be in evidence. I can't control the movement of the birds. And if I am too intent on seeing one particular bird, I may miss a lot of other things that are around. Prayer is like that:

Disclosure

Prayer is like watching for the
Kingfisher. All you can do is
Be where he is likely to appear, and
Wait.
Often, nothing much happens;
There is space, silence and
Expectancy.
No visible sign, only the
Knowledge that he's been there,
And may come again.
Seeing or not seeing cease to matter,
You have been prepared.
But sometimes, when you've almost
Stopped expecting it,
A flash of brightness
Gives encouragement.

So it's all gift. The work we have to do is be prepared, in the right habitat, with the right disposition. And then we have to respond, with thanksgiving for God's amazing love which cares even for the sparrows, endangered species that they are.

Kingfisher's glory, blackbird's song, the mystery of migration, the miracle of flight. And we are more precious. A mystery to ponder.

Surrounded by birds, where better to spend the day pondering?

Eucharistic Prayer
for a Quiet Garden event

(The words at the Sanctus and at the end of the prayer are taken from the hymn, Holy, Holy, Holy is the Lord.)

Creator God,
in whose garden our story began;
we praise and bless you for your continued
nurture and care as we grow in your kingdom.
We thank you for Jesus, who through his life,
death and resurrection opened the way
to fullness of life.
With angels and archangels, and all
who share in your life-giving love, we praise you,
singing:
Holy, holy, holy is the Lord,
holy is the Lord God almighty. *(Repeat)*
Who was, and is, and is to come.
Holy, holy, holy is the Lord.

Come to us now, holy God,
as we remember Jesus,
who on the night before he died
took bread and wine, blessed them
and gave them to his friends, saying,
'Eat and drink to remember me.'

Come freshly to us now, Lord God,
and bless these gifts of bread and wine.
As we receive them, may we be
rooted and grounded more deeply
in your love.
Nourish us with your life-giving Spirit,
and bring us at last to our full flowering,
where we shall glorify you for ever:

Glory, glory, glory to the Lord,
Glory to the Lord God almighty. *(Repeat)*
Who was, and is, and is to come.
Glory, glory, glory to the Lord.

Meditation for a Flower Festival

Jesus said, 'Consider ...'
Look steadily at the heart of what you contemplate;
be still, and know.

So we consider the flowers, their fragrance, their beauty, their perfection in simplicity.
We consider the flowers, and we give thanks to God for his great glory.

Let us bless the Lord:
Thanks be to God.

We consider the patience and tenacity of flowers – the years through which seeds lie dormant, until the time is right, the opportunity comes; perhaps through natural progression, perhaps through sudden upheaval, as when a motorway scars its way through the countryside, and the verges blaze with blood-red poppies.

We consider the flowers, and we give thanks to God for his patient love.

Let us bless the Lord:
Thanks be to God.

We consider the brokenness of flowers, through which new life comes. Unless the flower blooms and dies, it cannot produce seed; unless a seed dies, it cannot live, but when it falls to the ground and is broken open, new life begins.

We consider the flowers, and we give thanks to God for the life that he gives, through many deaths and resurrections making us whole.

Let us bless the Lord:
Thanks be to God.

We consider the flowers, and give thanks for the artistry and skill and hard work of those who have given us pleasure through this festival.

We consider the flowers, and we give thanks for all God's goodness.

Let us bless the Lord:
Thanks be to God.

We consider the flowers, and our own flowering: the pain and struggle with which our own creativity, in skills and relationships, gives birth and comes to fruition.

We consider the flowers, and we give thanks to God that places of darkness and pain as well as those of joy and light are places where his Spirit works.

Let us bless the Lord:
Thanks be to God.

We consider the flowers, and we give thanks for the way their shapes and colours and fragrances complement each other.

We consider the flowers, and we give thanks for the flowering of life in our community.

Let us bless the Lord:
Thanks be to God.

Planning a walk or a mini-pilgrimage

All over the world, through the centuries, people have gone on pilgrimage to holy places, for all sorts of reasons. A pilgrimage is about walking in someone else's footsteps, making someone else's story your own, asking about the significance of a place in God's eyes, becoming aware. It is often a journey made in the company of others, sharing memories and observations, a serious enterprise, and also fun.

You don't have to go to Mecca, or Jerusalem, or Canterbury. Our own localities have places of significance and people to remember too. All you need for a pilgrimage is some local knowledge, a bit of imagination, and, if possible, a few people to join you.

You don't need to draw attention to yourselves: a pilgrimage is not like a procession of witness, though other people may well be rather curious, and tag along.

You may want to use the walk to increase awareness of the goodness of God in creation. If that is the case, instead of remembering events of significance in the past, you could use the Benedicite (found in Morning Prayer in Anglican Prayer Books) as the basis for reflection.

Whatever the purpose, do the walk yourself first, and decide on the 'stations' – places to pause – and what you will do at each one. A useful pattern is:

- Stop and look.
- Listen to a reflection either about what you see now, or the significance of the place in the past.
- Pause for personal reflection.

- Pray together about the material you have been considering.

- Use a pilgrimage prayer which all can say – something like, 'Lord, keep us faithful and hopeful, and enable us to show your love in the world.'

- Walk on. It is not necessary to be silent on the walk – part of the value of a pilgrimage is that people become more aware of each other as well as God. Be ready for participants to make their own observations, too; you may well have a local historian or a naturalist in the group, and their contribution can add a great deal to the event.

Don't try to do too much – two and a half hours may be quite enough to tackle in a morning or an afternoon. Lunch could be part of the event, in which case try to arrange for a suitable place to have it, either provided by someone not on the walk, or a picnic. End with a 'cuppa' – it is important to share food and drink on these occasions.

You may wish to end in a church or hall or someone's home, and spend a few minutes reflecting on the experience, noting where and how God was present to you.

Make it clear in the publicity what kind of event it will be, and arrange an alternative activity in case of rain. It would be possible to set the 'stations' in a church if the weather is inclement. Simon Bailey's book, *Stations*, has some imaginative ideas for a pilgrimage round your church, town, home or body, depending on your degree of mobility. No one need be excluded, but you do need to be realistic about what people can manage physically.

Eucharistic Prayer for city dwellers

Lord of all life,
whose disciples were told
to wait in the city
until they were empowered by your Spirit;
we thank you for our calling to be in this city,
to recognize and name your power
in obvious and unlikely places.
With people on many different paths of faith
who seek the common good, we praise you, saying:
Holy and life-giving God,
vulnerable and strong,
all you have made is full of your glory,
all praise to your name.

Come freshly to us, living God.
Free us from the fear that the task
will be too great;
encourage us with signs of your presence,
and nourish us with the life of your Son,
who, on the night before he died,
took bread and wine, blessed them
and gave them to his disciples, saying,
'This is my body given for you.
This is my blood shed for you.
Do this to remember me.'

Come then, Lord,
and make yourself known in our streets,
that our city may dance with your life,
and its heart beat with
the power of your love. **Amen.**

Give us this day – Lammas Day

August begins with Lammas Day, Loaf Mass Day, the day in the *Book of Common Prayer* calendar when a loaf baked with flour from newly harvested corn would be brought into church and blessed. It's one of the oldest points of contact between the agricultural world and the Church. The others were Plough Sunday in early January, the Sunday after Epiphany and the day before work would begin again in the fields after the Christmas festivities, when the ploughs would be brought to church to be blessed; and Rogation days in May, the days before Ascension Day, when God's blessing would be sought on the growing crops. Farming communities have always celebrated the successful gathering in of harvest, but our church observance of Harvest Festival was only introduced in the nineteenth century. Perhaps Lammas Day served that purpose in earlier generations.

One of the things I decided to do when I retired was to learn to make bread. I'd made several attempts over the years which had produced something edible (because the ingredients were edible) but nothing I would have offered to share with others. But with the help of a friend who showed me what to do, I had another go. And I became fascinated by the process. Modern bread-making machines turn out a decent loaf, but there is nothing quite like the hands-on experience.

One of the fascinating things about it is the yeast: that unprepossessing lump of putty-like substance, or even more unlikely looking granules of dried yeast. Give yeast warmth and sugar and liquid, and miraculously it grows before your eyes. And then it makes the dough rise and double its size. It seems irrepressible. Knock the dough down, and leave it to its own devices, and it will double its size again.

In the Middle Ages, one of the names for yeast was 'goddisgoode' – written as one word as though it were God's e-mail address – because, people said, 'it cometh of the grete grece (sic) of God'. No one understood its chemistry, or knew its origin, it was a gift from God. Like manna of Old Testament times, pure gift. God is good. That is what lies at the heart of bread.

When Jesus said that he is the Bread of Life, embodied for us now in the Eucharist, he was offering himself as a gift as fundamental to meeting our inner needs as bread is to meeting our physical needs. Through feeding on him, God gives us himself, and that is all we need.

But that isn't the end of it. Jesus used yeast as one of his illustrations about the way the kingdom of God works. And when he gave himself as bread, he said it was for the life of the world (John 6.51). We share God's life so that we can *be* the truth that God is good.

God is good. World events and the circumstances of our lives will often knock that truth about, knock it down as dough is knocked down. But God's goodness is irrepressible, and the warmth of our response will help people to recognize it. That's the heart of evangelism: to help people to know the goodness of God. People outside the Church, and some within it, too, judging by some of the debates we've been having recently, seem to think that the Christian life is all about having a set of rules to live by – not a very life-enhancing approach. Jesus offers us something more deeply satisfying, the Bread of Life which assures us that God is good, and meets our deepest needs.

Christians are not people who occupy the high moral ground, who have got the answers to all life's problems. As the Indian evangelist D.T. Niles has said, 'Evangelism is witness. It is one beggar telling another beggar where to get food'. The task of evangelism is to share the good news of God's goodness, and invite others to enjoy the Bread of Life too.

Prayers at a wedding

Loving God,
we give thanks with N and N
for all the people who have loved and cared for them,
challenged and encouraged them
in their lives so far.
We pray that you will give them the grace
that they need,
as they shape their lives together in marriage:
may they give each other space,
and support each other with sensitivity;
may they meet difficulties with courage and humour,
and enjoy the good times with thankfulness;
may their friendships and their hospitality
spring always from deep commitment to each other
and to you;
and may they continue to grow
in knowledge and experience of
the riches of your love.
We ask this in the name of Christ. **Amen.**

Gracious God,
you call us all to be channels of your grace;
may we who are witnesses to this marriage
support N and N in their life together:
may we set them free from old expectations
to live their life in increasing joy;
may we be ready to listen,
and generous in our understanding;
give us wisdom to know when to speak
and when to be silent;
may N and N find in us
resources of friendship
appropriate to their need.

Come freshly to us all, Lord God:
keep us faithful to your call,
that in all our relationships
we may be signs
of your kingdom of peace and love;
and so we pray:
Our Father ....

Suggestion for an introduction to a marriage service after a divorce

With the bride and groom standing at the front of the church, facing each other, but apart, the minister addresses the congregation:

Minister: N and N have come to celebrate their marriage, (each) with memories of a previous relationship. They want, as they prepare to make their vows to each other, to give thanks for all that was good in those partnerships (*especially their children), to acknowledge responsibility for their own part in the breakdown of their first marriage, and to ask forgiveness for their own personal failures to live in love.

Minister, addressing N and N:

N and N, you have talked with each other, and faced as honestly as you can the reasons for the breakdown of your previous relationships. Each of you is loved by God, and nothing you have done has put you beyond that love. You, like all of us, need assurance that God's love is greater than our failures, and I invite you now to open yourselves again to the healing power of God's forgiveness.**

Silence

We say together:

> **Compassionate God,**
> **come to us and heal us;**
> **forgive our failures to love,**
> **and free us from guilt**
> **about what is past.**
> **Help us to love and serve you**
> **wholeheartedly**
> **in our new relationship**
> **with each other.**

Minister: God in his mercy sets us free.
Take hold of this forgiveness
and live your lives together
in joy and freedom in God's love. **Amen.**

* omit if there are no children

** At this point the minister could add something along these lines:

N and N have identified their particular need, but we all stand in need of forgiveness, and all of us can join in these words, whether aloud or in our hearts, and receive God's forgiveness.

Prayers for the blessing of a house

As participants walk round the house, it would be appropriate to sing the Taizé chant 'Ubi Caritas'. Candles may be lit at each 'station'.

At the front door
Lord God, in Jesus Christ, you came and shared the life of an ordinary home. May this house always be a place of welcome. Bless all who come here, and all who receive them, that they may enter in love, and go out with joy. **Amen.**

In the kitchen
Lord, you are the bread of life. May all who prepare food and offer hospitality here know your presence and be sustained by your peace. **Amen.**

In the dining room
Lord, you make yourself known in the breaking of bread. May all who share fellowship at this table be filled with your life. **Amen.**

In the study
Lord, you have the words of life. May all who read and think and join in conversation here be filled with your wisdom, and be led to your truth. **Amen.**

In a quiet room
In quietness and confidence is our strength. May all who come to this room find your peace and encouragement. **Amen.**

In the sitting room
Where two or three are gathered together in your name, Lord, you are there. May all who use this room be assured of your presence. **Amen.**

On the stairs
Lord, you invited your disciples to come apart from the busy demands of life. May we be refreshed and cleansed, and enjoy your gift of sleep. **Amen.**

In the garden
Lord God, you walked in the garden in the cool of the day, and in a garden your Son was first known to be risen from the dead. May this garden be a place of peace and refreshment for all who work and relax in it. **Amen.**

Eucharistic Prayer at a house blessing

Lord God,
we praise you for calling us
to be the household of faith;
and for blessing us with
companions to encourage us
in our loving;
we praise you for giving us gifts
sufficient for our needs,
and in generous measure
to share with our neighbours.
With angels and archangels
and all who through the ages
have responded to your call,
we rejoice and sing:
Holy, holy, holy Lord,
God of life and joy,
Heaven and earth are full of your glory,
Hosanna in the highest.

Come now, Lord, and make your dwelling
in our hearts and homes,
as we remember Jesus, who
on the night before his death,
took bread and wine, blessed them
and gave them to his friends, saying,
'This is my body given for you.
This is my blood shed for you.
Eat and drink to remember me.'

As we share your life in this bread and this cup,
may we, with all the faithful in this place,
be set aflame with your love,
and filled with your power,
that others may see
and be drawn to you,
and live to your glory and praise. **Amen.**

At a baptism

Jesus said, 'I am the way, the truth and the life.'

Before the name 'Christian' was used, in the early years of the Church's life, followers of Jesus were known as people of the Way.

As you grow up, and begin to discover what it means to live the Jesus Way, you might like to ponder these truths, which we who were present at your baptism pass on to you.

First, you are precious to God (Isaiah 43.4). Nothing you can do, no circumstances of your life can alter that. You may turn away from God, but God will never stop loving you, and will always welcome you back.

Then, you have a relationship with the created world. 'Consider the birds,' Jesus said (Matthew 6.26). Look at the flowers, marvel at the wonders of the created world, and the sustaining power of God which holds them in life. Let them remind you of your value. But being chosen and special does not mean being spoilt. We have a responsibility to the created world, and your relationship with God will challenge you to care for all that is around you, and use it with respect.

That leads to your relationship with people around you. They also are precious to God, and people who are on the Jesus Way are called to treat others as people who are loved, honoured and precious like us.

There will always be people on the Jesus Way to encourage you as you join in worship, read the Bible and learn to pray and reflect on your relationship with God and the world. But deeper than that is the love of God sustaining you, and the energy and life of

God's Spirit filling you, and the friendship of Jesus as he walks with us all on the Way.

Have a good journey!

Eucharistic Prayer
celebrating family life

Father of all,
we praise you that you have shown us
in the earthly life of your Son,
how love is nurtured and grown
in the testing ground of family life:
Help us to be faithful in our loving.

We praise you that in Jesus,
now risen and glorified,
you offer us fullness of life
beyond our imagining:
Raise us to life with him.

We praise you for the Spirit's
surprising presence, urging us on
to explore the riches of your love:
Open our hearts to your transforming power.

Open us up to your glory, Lord, as
with angels and archangels and
all who through the ages
have responded to your call,
we praise you, saying:
Holy, holy, holy Lord,
God of love and joy;
Heaven and earth are full of your glory,
all praise to your name.

Come now, Lord, and make your dwelling
in our hearts and homes,
as we remember Jesus, who
on the night before his death,
took bread and wine, blessed them
and gave them to his friends, saying,

'This is my body, given for you.
This is my blood, shed for you.
Eat and drink to remember me.'

Come freshly to us, living God,
and through these gifts of bread and wine
nourish us with your life.

In all the changes we experience
steady us with your faithfulness.

In all our relationships
inspire us with your love.

May our families and our homes
be signs of your kingdom:
**Your kingdom come in us, Lord,
and transform the world
to your praise and glory. Amen.**

Harvest

Celebrating harvest goes very deep in us – it seems to stir in us a sense of our country roots, memories of a land that lived by agriculture before the Industrial Revolution turned most of us into townies. Some of us don't have to go very far back to find our farming connections. My mother was a farmer's daughter, and she talked about the Harvest Home celebrations, when the big table that our branch of the family inherited was connected by a spare leaf to another like it, and all at the farm marked the end of the harvest with a party.

Although none of us has done it, probably, we sing 'We plough the fields and scatter the good seed on the land', and it doesn't seem in the least odd, even though farmers are much more efficient in their methods now. Harvest marks the end of a sequence in the church/country calendar. Plough Sunday in January, when the farm implements were blessed; Rogation Days just before Ascension Day in May, when prayers were made for favourable weather for the growing crops; Lammas Day at the beginning of August, when the first loaf made with flour from the new crop was offered in token thanks, and coming full circle, (though it was introduced much later on the liturgical scene, in the nineteenth century) Harvest. Time for a pause before it all starts again. Time to be thankful, to remember God's mercy and goodness, enjoying the sight of full storehouses and barns, pantry shelves and freezers. Time to feel secure against the coming winter. It is good to be thankful, and we come gladly, enjoying the colour, the smells and, with luck, a party.

But there's something uncomfortable about Harvest, too, especially now that we can see on our television screens that there are people who haven't got a harvest to celebrate, some who haven't had a harvest for years, perhaps because the rains have failed, perhaps because civil wars have made it impossible to cultivate the land. The Jewish people faced the same situation on a smaller scale. Reading the instructions in Deuteronomy we are reminded that God's people have always been told to be generous and help the poor to share our good fortune. Deuteronomy speaks of very different farming methods, but the message is clear: don't keep it all to yourself, leave something for those in need.

And the New Testament warns us against taking things for granted, being pleased with our achievement. That man who pulled down his barn and built a bigger one, stuffed it full and sat back feeling pleased with himself got a sharp reminder – 'You fool! This very night your life is being demanded of you. And the things you have prepared, whose will they be?' (Luke 12.16-21). That's the question Harvest asks us too.

In the Bible, harvest and judgement go together – the parable of the wheat and the tares puts the point very starkly (Matthew 13.24-30). So it's right and good to be thankful, but we have to ask ourselves how our thankfulness can find expression in making it possible for all humankind to be thankful. We can't ever sit back and say we've done enough – not while there are all those children with stick limbs and swollen bellies looking at us hopelessly from our screens.

If we are going to be on the side of the angels, we have to work for the elimination of hunger, and the inhumanity which locks most of the world's food away from those who need it most. We have to support the agencies who work to improve farming methods, but we also need to put our political will behind the removal of world debt, an issue which keeps on being pushed down the agenda by scandals and atrocities across the world. We must keep asking the questions and seeking action. Harvest is the point where, far from sitting back and thinking how fortunate we are, we have to prepare to sow the seeds and encourage the growth for the harvest to come, when the will of God will be done on earth, as it is in heaven.

St Michael and All Angels

Would you recognize an angel if you saw one? I suppose we all think we would, because we've seen pictures of them so often. Painters and sculptors have given us the conventions: wings, floating robes, haloes. So we know how to portray even the most un-angelic if we want them to be angels: children look so different when dressed for the part. But we only have to see them out of costume, being children, to recognise that the stage props can be misleading.

Perhaps we come closer to recognizing an angel when we say, in response to an act of kindness, 'Oh, you are an angel!' Or to persuade someone to do an act of kindness we say, 'Be an angel.' But the Bible opens our eyes to angelic presence with a harder edge, and in more guises than we have always recognized.

Angels

Flames of fire, shafts of illumination;
Disconcerting messengers of God;
Assuring a woman that she can give birth;
Telling a man that what she bears is
Gift from God; challenging us to
Look, and not seek life where only death
Is found; opening doors, surrounding us with
Care, surprising us into fresh understanding.

Since about 500 AD, the heavenly host has been divided into nine 'Orders', in three groups of three. In the top rank are the *Seraphim*, the six-winged creatures whose work is the praise of God, ceaselessly chanting, 'Holy, holy, holy' (Isaiah 6.3). They are accompanied by the *Cherubim*, guardians of the truth and the presence of God. Cherubim (the word is plural) were stationed at the gateway to Eden, to guard the way to the tree of life, and placed at each end of the Ark of the Covenant to guard the place where God was thought to be specially present. They were strong creatures, with no resemblance to the *putti* beloved of baroque artists (Genesis 3.24; Exodus 25.18-22; 2 Samuel 22.10-13; Psalm 18.10; 80.1; 99.1). The third group in this first rank were called *Thrones*, the great wheels or many-eyed ones, sometimes acting as chariots. There's a description of their likeness in Ezekiel's vision of the appearance of God at the beginning of his book (Ezekiel 1). And when Elisha's servant got frightened in battle, Elisha prayed that his eyes would be opened, and he saw the chariots of fire surrounding the armies, out-numbering the enemy by far (2 Kings 6.17).

In the middle group of three are *Dominions*, (angels of mercy) *Virtues* (angels of blessing) and *Powers* (on the borders of heaven guarding against demonic intervention). These are only mentioned in passing in Scripture, but were part of ancient thinking.

In the last group are *Principalities*, originally protectors of nations and cities, and the *Archangels* and *Angels*, the two Orders which have direct dealings with humans.

Sanctus

Should you hear them singing among stars
or whispering secrets of a wiser world,
do not imagine ardent fledgling children.
They are intelligences old as sunrise
that never learnt left from right,
    before from after,
knowing but one direction, into God,
    but one duration, now.

Their melody strides not from bar to bar,
but like a painting hangs there entire
one chord of limitless communication.
You have heard it in the rhythms of the hills,
the spiralling turn of a dance, the
    fall of words
or the touch of fingers at the right,
    rare moment,
and these were holy, holy.

                      (John V. Taylor)

We know the names of three Archangels from the Bible: Michael, remembered for his great battle against evil (Daniel 10.13, 12.1; Revelation 12.7-9); Gabriel who played such an active part in the events surrounding Jesus' birth (Luke 1 and 2); and Raphael concerned with healing (Tobit 3.17). Uriel is named in Jewish tradition. Other traditions name Metatron and Azael. There seem to have been seven Archangels, but the names of the remaining three vary in different traditions.

The Angels are those who have most dealings with humans. The word 'angel' means 'messenger', and the Angels are around in the biblical story surprising people into new understanding of God's ways with humanity. They are not always immediately recognized, and they bring challenge as well as comfort. They move with ease between earth and heaven, putting their worship into practice by ensuring that God's purposes are carried out on earth (Genesis 18.1-16; 28.10-17; Numbers 22 and 23; Matthew 13.37-42, 47-50; 18.10; Acts 10.1-8; 12.1-11; 27.21-25; Hebrews 13.2; Revelation 5.11-14).

It is in the company of all these heavenly beings that we live our lives, and they challenge us in our commitment. There is no doubt where their priority lies: it is in worship. But worship is only complete when the whole of existence is directed to putting God first. We are caught up in the continuing conflict between good and evil: events around us provide plenty of evidence that evil is alive and rotten in our world. But our faith is that the power of love and good is stronger, and we are invited to join the work of the Angels by putting that faith into practice. We are called to challenge oppression and injustice, and to work for peace. These sound like global politics, and so they are. But they are also the stuff of ordinary life, as we interact with our fellow humans.

The Angels are God's messengers, listening for God's word, and acting on it. We are invited to join them in their listening, and then help those around us to hear as well. The Angels are symbols of God's continuing care for his creation, care in which we are also involved.

Angels are part of the poetry of God's love. Poetry doesn't define or prescribe, but opens our eyes to new understanding. Lord, open our minds and our hearts, and keep us faithful in your love.

(Ideas from the preceding reflection can be developed into a workshop, using art, music and poetry, and providing opportunity for creative work, both in artistic areas and in looking at involvement in work for peace and justice.)

Suffering

Suffering is probably the biggest challenge our faith will encounter. We are all puzzled by it, have difficulty in making sense of it, fear it, resent it, and wonder where, if at all, it fits into God's will.

None of us escapes suffering. We experience loss and pain, and we watch others suffer too, whether remotely, through the awful pictures on TV of starving, homeless people in Africa or war-torn countries in Europe and the Middle East, or in our own families as illness or despair, or loss of independence in the diminishments of old age, bite deeper. We want to know *why*? We want to know how long it's going to go on. We hate the feeling that we're not in control.

Like many people, I've struggled with these questions, and wrestled with God in the pain of human experience. Perhaps, though, the most important thing is not what we end up saying about suffering, but what we end up saying about God.

There is a deep-seated strand of thinking that persists in saying that God sends suffering to test us. I find that hard to square with the God revealed in Jesus Christ, who made it quite plain that suffering is *not* what God wants. Jesus *healed* the sick, *challenged* the people who oppressed others. 'I came that [people] may have life,' he said (John 10.10).

Nor is it easy to square what we know of God in Jesus with another prevalent idea, that somehow we deserve what we get. We rebel almost instinctively against that thought – 'What have I done to deserve this?' we say. The answer is usually, 'nothing'. Of course, there is suffering we bring on ourselves – but it is a consequence of *our* actions, rather than a punishment from God. How can those starving children in Africa deserve such suffering? How have victims of murder come to deserve their fate? Some suffering is caused by sin, but it is not the sin of those who suffer, but the sin of those who hold life cheap.

So, if suffering is not a test, and not something we deserve, why does it happen, and why doesn't God do something to prevent it? This question was focused for me very sharply during the years when I was caring for my mother as she moved further and further into the confusion of senile dementia. She ceased to be the person we had known; she didn't know who she was, or who anyone else was, and the disintegration was awful to watch. Her freedom and wholeness, and ours, would only come through death – but she showed no signs of dying.

One day, while she was struggling with this existence, as I walked to work, a man dropped dead in front of me. I learnt during the day that he was a man in his fifties, who had left a widow, and two sons just about to start at university. Where was the sense in that death? There was my mother still going on in her twilight existence, and this man who had gone out to work that morning apparently with quite a lot of useful life ahead of him, suddenly dead. It seemed a cruel irony.

'You must be left with some questions,' said a friend when I told him what had happened. True, but in the end it was only one question. Did God know what he was doing? I've already said that I don't believe God sends suffering as a test or for any other reason. I desperately wanted God to intervene and put an end to my mother's suffering. But that raised another problem, because I don't believe in that sort of God either. God has given the universe laws which it has to follow, and there was no reason why they should be varied for me or for my mother. I did not doubt that God was in it all somewhere; the question was, where? (It is, of course, more complex than that, because God does sometimes apparently intervene!)

Gradually I came to a fresh understanding. I had been brought up with a vocabulary which only used words like almighty, powerful, omnipotent, in connection with God. I needed new words, like vulnerable, and suffering. An all-powerful God who makes people suffer, or who acts capriciously, would not be a God worth worshipping. But a God who has made himself vulnerable by offering us responsibility, and giving us free will; who suffers with us, and is brought to his knees with us, and who continually brings new life out of dead ends, that's a God I can relate to. Not obviously omnipotent, but skilled in crisis management. God's will is that people should be whole, and his will is constantly thwarted by illness, suffering, loss and death. And in all this, God suffers too, helping us to bear the pain and find signs of hope.

So when I in turn became ill, I felt that God and I had been here before, in a situation not of his will, and certainly not my choice, and that the way through was to hang on to God's faithfulness, in it with me, sharing the pain, holding me in love. Perhaps that's what taking up our cross means: being faithful to our commitment to the God we worship, finding God in the midst of whatever life throws at us.

'Christ in you, the hope of glory' (Colossians 1.27). We read those words sometimes in a triumphalist way, as though we've already got to the glory. But Paul was writing about hope, which always relates to something ahead of us. And he wrote it in the context of our suffering being part of Christ's suffering. It is the Christ who suffered and stayed faithful whom we meet in our pain. In his brokenness, in Gethsemane and the cross, he speaks to our vulnerability and calls us to himself. We can never say, 'God, you don't know what it's like to suffer.' In Jesus, God shows us that he does know.

Prayer for healing

'I came that they may have life, and have it abundantly' (John 10.10).

We all long for that, but how do we achieve it? Some people put their trust in something like the Lottery – fullness of life, they say, will be possible when we can pay off all our debts and buy all we want. But those who pray for healing acknowledge that there are deeper needs than those for which money can provide. Good though it might be to be out of debt, able to do what we want without having to go without something else, deep down we know that we have other needs.

The ministry of prayer for healing and wholeness is a way of addressing those needs which the Church has encouraged right from the early days. James 5.13-16 indicates that this ministry was a part of Church practice from an early stage. It sprang out of a realization that healing lay at the heart of Jesus' ministry, as he healed physical and emotional pain, eased strained relationships with forgiveness, and encouraged people to realize that God's love is stronger than whatever may be disturbing us.

But what is healing? It is probably helpful to recognize that it is not necessarily the same as a cure. In some Christian traditions, you would expect to find a heap of crutches or hearing aids left behind after a service of prayer for healing, because they were no longer necessary. That may happen, but if it doesn't, it won't mean that healing hasn't taken place.

I learnt most about the difference between healing and cure when my father was diagnosed with cancer. At first I prayed very hard that he would get better. But his cancer was too far advanced for that, and however hard I prayed, it soon became obvious that he was going to die – and the longer he lived, the more he would suffer. Gradually my prayer changed, as I began to realize that for him, healing would only come through death. And perhaps that's always the truth, that only death will give us the freedom to be truly whole. It wasn't easy to accept. I often felt very angry. And part of my healing was to realize that it is all right to be angry with God. God is big enough to take it – that's part of what the cross is about.

God was at work then, changing my father, changing me, changing the family, leading us all on to something new. Although there was no cure (my father died), I'm sure there was healing. It showed in my father's courage in facing pain and death; it showed in the way we as a family were drawn closer together and began to be able to express our love for each other more openly; it showed in the way we were set free from fear and anxiety. That doesn't mean that his death didn't hurt – it was a painful letting go all round. But it led on to something new. Healing doesn't mean going back to what one was before, it's a growing on to a new stage. It can be painful and costly as the growth takes us through many deaths and resurrections on our way to life.

Healing may take us by surprise – after one healing service I attended, a woman who was going blind said, 'I know I'm going blind, but after tonight, I'm not so afraid.' Prayer for healing means opening ourselves up to God's love, asking God to give us what God knows we need, rather than putting a lot of energy into asking for what we want. We might do well to remember those four men who brought their paralysed friend to Jesus, with energy that let nothing stand in their way (Mark 2.1-12). No doubt they wanted their friend to walk again but, wisely, they didn't restrict Jesus' actions by saying so. They let

Jesus deal with what lay at the root of the man's illness, and Jesus set him free from whatever it was that had left him helpless, literally without a leg to stand on, for so long.

So, we come asking for healing, perhaps knowing our need, perhaps with a sense of need we can't put into words. Or we might come because, like those four men, we want to bring someone else to Jesus for his healing touch. We might come in gratitude that we are being healed, with a longing that our spiritual life will be strengthened and deepened.

The result of our prayer will be an expression of God's love for us. It may be the disappearance of whatever is troubling us, it may be a new appreciation of our own worth; it may be a new determination to work for social changes that will bring wholeness to others; it may be fresh courage to face an old situation. We may not be aware that anything has happened until later. But God will respond with his healing gifts at whatever level we can receive them. And then we go out to offer his healing to those around us, for healing is not just for individuals. I can't be whole while my brothers and sisters in the world are in need. Part of the healing we must pray for is that society, ours and others', and our church communities too, will change so that all people will be free to find their wholeness. Part of our wholeness will come as we work for the peace, freedom and justice which are God's will for us all.

Give thanks –always?

Thank you. That's one of the first things children learn to say. And it's fine when we can see what it is we have to be thankful for. One of the things I remember from my childhood was writing thank-you letters. Christmas and birthdays brought lots of gifts, but the downside was writing the letters in response. I don't know whether children still go through the same discipline – it's so easy to pick up the phone, or let mum or dad do it for you.

I was quite happy to write when the gift was something I appreciated, but it wasn't so easy when the donor didn't seem to have remembered who I was. One of my aunts always caused difficulties. She sent me a doll's hot water bottle once, apparently unaware that I was 12 years old that birthday!

Saying thank you can be problematic – you probably know the series of letters by John Julius Norwich, purporting to have been written by Emily to Edward in response to the gifts sent on the 12 days of Christmas, ending with a broken engagement, and a solicitor's letter restraining Edward from sending further gifts.

Against that background of experience, we find ourselves reminded to give thanks to God the Father at all times and for everything in the name of our Lord Jesus Christ (Ephesians 5.20). When we count our blessings, we find that there are far more than we thought. But that isn't the whole of our experience. How do we thank God when we are in the middle of one of those awful patches when it doesn't look as though there is much to be thankful for: when life falls apart at the death of a loved one, or the loss of a job; when health deserts us, or hospital tests hang over us; when life loses its meaning, or the world situation seems so dire that we can't see much hope for the future?

What we can always give thanks for is God's faithfulness, holding us through all the darknesses and difficulties. We are not told to perform extraordinary emotional or mental gymnastics to persuade ourselves that somehow everything that happens is for the best. Jesus never gave the impression that somehow suffering would be good for us: he healed the sick, opposed all that destroyed people's lives, whether inner forces or those of society.

Jesus also made it clear that sometimes the only way to deal with suffering is to go through it and find, as he did at the end, that God has been holding us all the time. God's faithfulness to his people led him to enter into their suffering and pain, throughout their history but supremely in his engagement with the world in Jesus. We can never say, 'It's all right for you, God, you don't know what it's like.' God does know, he's in our circumstances, whatever they are, holding us in his profound love. And that is what we give thanks for, at all times and in all places.

One of the heroes of the Church is Polycarp, a bishop in Asia in the second century. He was martyred during one of the fiercest persecutions the Church experienced. When it became clear that the Roman officials were after him, he wanted to stay in the city and face them. His friends persuaded him to leave, and he went to a farm not far from the city, and spent his time in prayer, not for himself but, as his custom was, for the people of the world, and the churches in their mission to them. His respite was short-lived, and his pursuers caught up with him quite late on a Friday evening. Polycarp ordered that they should be given food and drink, and asked that they should give him an hour for prayer. In fact he prayed for two hours, and those who witnessed his prayer began to feel ashamed that they had come after so venerable an old man.

He was taken back to the city and, throughout the journey, his captors tried to persuade him to say, 'Caesar is Lord', and save himself. But he refused even to think of it. He was brought to the stadium and asked formally to swear allegiance to Caesar and curse Christ. Polycarp's response was to say, 'Eighty-six years I have served him, and he has done me no wrong. How then can I blaspheme my king who saved me?' So he was martyred.

'Eighty-six years I have served him, and he has done me no wrong.' We can all say that, whatever our age. God has done me no wrong. At all times and in all places, God's love never fails. That's the fact to hang on to, the reason for ever-growing thankfulness.

Remember, Remember, the theme of November

We remember many people in November: All Saints, All Souls, Guy Fawkes and, on Remembrance Day, all who have given their lives in war.

The festival of All Saints reminds us that we are part of a great company of people who have been touched by God, and have responded by living lives that in some measure give God glory. Saints are not extraordinarily holy people, so heavenly minded that they are no earthly use: weak, rather silly looking, with stained glass haloes like dinner plates. All of us who have given our lives to God, however tentatively, are called saints in the New Testament. Look at the beginnings of Paul's letters, and think about what we know of the recipients. Take the Corinthians, for example, a more quarrelsome lot of people it would be hard to find. They argued amongst themselves and with Paul; they competed with each other about which were the best gifts to have, and which was the best leader to follow; they held services which were hardly a model of decorum; and they found it very difficult to work out how to apply their new faith to public life. Saints just like us, in fact.

Then comes the remembrance of All Souls, with the reminder that we are not only concerned with time and space, but with life beyond. Death is not 'nothing at all' as a popular reading at funerals suggests. Death is a very significant part of our life, which separates us, like birth at our beginning, from whatever lies beyond our conscious experience. All Souls Day is when we remember all those who have lived their lives and moved *on*, not *away*, but out of the spotlight.

We often think of time in a linear way. Bede records the conversation between Edwin, King of Northumbria in the seventh century, and his advisers when he was considering whether to adopt the Christian faith. One of the advisers, gesturing to the feasting hall in which they were assembled, with a central fire burning and unglazed windows gaping on to the darkness outside, suggested that human life is like that of a sparrow which flies into the feasting hall. For a short time it is in the light, but we don't know where it has come from or where it goes when it leaves. If this new faith tells us anything about the unseen world around us, then it is worth exploring (Bede *Ecclesiastical History* ch. XIII).

If we change the imagery from a line to a series of concentric circles, then our life is more like being on stage at a performance in the round, with all the people who have played their part, and those in the wings waiting to come on, watching with interest and some sympathy as we try to make sense of the script we have been given. And at the end, when the lights come up, we find the author of life's play is there to commend us, or perhaps to make a few suggestions about how our performance could have been improved. All Souls Day reminds us of the unseen audience, some of whom we know and love for the way they have influenced our lives, for whom we give thanks along with all the others whom we don't know, but who share with us in God's love.

So we can be encouraged as we think of this great cloud of witnesses surrounding us on our journey, and renew our commitment to persevere in the race that lies ahead, looking to Jesus as we go (Hebrews 12.1-2).

Death – terminus or junction?

Ad Quem

Death – terminus,
Heart-stopping jolt
At the end of the line?
Or junction, where worlds meet,
Faith catching the connection?

The one certain thing about us is that we will die. But we don't talk about death unless we have to. In our society we are cushioned from its reality. In spite of the number of violent deaths we see on our TV screens, many people have never seen or touched a dead person; and we keep being assured that steps are being taken to cut down the number of deaths from particular diseases, as though that will mean that some of us won't die at all.

It is good to work at eliminating pain and suffering, and it is natural to feel outrage at premature or violent death. But we seem to have great difficulty in accepting that death is a natural part of life. We have moved a long way from awareness of the natural rhythms of nature. Every year, the seasons remind us of new life growing to maturity and then moving towards death. Observation of the life of trees and plants teaches us that in order for life to continue, it has to progress from one stage to the next. A flower has to die before seed can be set. The seeds have to fall from the plant, apparently dead, before the next cycle of life can begin.

When I was a small child, I used to be puzzled when we prayed in church for people who were dangerously ill. In danger of what, I wondered. Presumably they were in danger of dying. But I also heard in church that there was something called eternal life, which seemed to be on the other side of death. Many years and experiences have intervened, and I've realized that things aren't that simple. Apart from the suffering that sometimes precedes death, there is always pain at the loss of people we love, and there are questions about what happens to us when we die.

Canon Henry Scott Holland, in a sermon preached at the Lying-in-State of Edward VII, said that we hover between two ways of regarding death. One is that death is the end. We recoil from this death, and protest at it, for it is unbearable to think that we shall never be able to talk to our loved ones, or touch them, again. Death is an insuperable barrier. The other view is that death is nothing at all. The person we loved is no longer there in the coffin in front of us, but they still exist. We go on thinking about them, praying for them, remembering them. This passage from the sermon is often read at funerals. It begins with the words 'Death is nothing at all.' But taken out of context, the passage is a denial of the reality we are experiencing when we are bereaved. Scott Holland went on to say that we may try to deny the fact of death, because it is so painful. But the sense of unreality we sometimes feel as we look at a dead body and realize that the person we loved is no longer there, will give way to the realization that far from being nothing at all, death is a hard reality which has made a difference. Our task, he said, is to reconcile both views of death: it is an end, but there is a continuity of growth in the love of God which enables this end to be a new beginning. The sermon was preached at Pentecost, and the preacher reminded his hearers that the gift of the Spirit was the gift of God's life experienced now, so that eternal life is not only life beyond the grave, but a life we begin to live here and now.

When we begin to grasp that idea, we have a new insight to offer. Death is not the worst thing that can happen to us. It is, rather, a natural stage in our growth. In the imagery of the poem at the beginning of this reflection, it is not a terminus but a junction, where worlds meet.

It is faith that catches the connection – and faith is not the same as certainty. Faith is an attitude of trust in the God who is always faithful. We learn that trust through many experiences of letting go in order that new life may grow. There are many deaths and resurrections on the way to fullness of life.

We don't know when we shall die – but we can prepare for it. 'From *sudden* death, Good Lord, deliver us' is a prayer (from the *Book of Common Prayer*), that we will be spared an *unprepared* death. There are, of course, practical things we can do to prepare for death, like making a will, and keeping our affairs in order so that our executors don't have too hard a task. But the deeper preparation lies in attending to our relationship with God, practising God's presence in our lives, making full use of the gift of life which is ours now, and which will grow into its fullness in God's love.

Year's mind

Every year, I pass the day
Not knowing. Someday
Someone will say, 'Oh yes,
Ann died a year ago.'

I pray they will remember
A day when I lived to the full,
A day of celebration
Of the gift of life.

Remembrance Day

Remembrance Day calls us to memories of the dead of two world wars, and the 60 or so years since of anything but peace. The numbers are mind-blowing, as we think of Africa, Europe, Ireland, the Middle East, in our lifetime. It has been said that if all who died in the First World War marched four abreast, when the head of the column reached the Cenotaph, the end would be at Durham; at the end of the Second War at Edinburgh. Who knows where it would be now? And we remember not just the dead, but all who have suffered the living death of mental torture or physical disability.

Each year, as the time for remembrance comes round, very mixed emotions surface. For some, the pain and suffering they experience is still so great that all commemoration is tinged with bitterness. Talk of reconciliation and forgiveness provokes anger, and a feeling that no one understands the horror and brutality they witnessed or experienced. For others, the commemoration is the opportunity to acknowledge the horror of war, and pay tribute to those who sacrificed themselves, or were sacrificed, and to express gratitude for the measure of co-operation that has been achieved between nations who were formerly at each other's throats.

Others find themselves close to despair, because people seem to have learned so little. We've seen history repeating itself in the Balkans; we've seen a peace process that was conceived in such hope in Northern Ireland almost destroyed by people who can't let go of ancient feuds; we've seen unspeakable cruelty in parts of Africa; and then there's Afghanistan, and Iraq, and the Middle East. The list could go on. And it won't include only things that happen outside the UK. What has happened to the vision of 'a world fit for heroes to live in' we ask, as we look at the homeless, the helpless, the despised in our own society.

What is the point of remembering if we don't learn from what we remember? It has been said that history repeats itself because we don't learn the lessons the first time round. Remembering has to be coupled with action for a better world. One of the tasks the gospel calls us to is that of peacemaking. That can sound very bland, pouring oil on troubled waters, pretending that as long as everything looks all right on the surface, all is well.

To be a peacemaker is to be at the cutting edge of relationships, where, as we draw closer together in our common humanity, we take forgiveness seriously. One of the first things to recognize about forgiveness is that we all need it. None of us belongs to a race with absolutely clean hands. All participants in war do terrible things to each other. We have to stop looking for someone else to blame, and look at where our responsibility lies. We have to recognize that within each of us there is the potential for evil as well as for good – and if we haven't behaved all that badly as individuals, let's give thanks that the grace of God has been at work in us.

What, then, is forgiveness? We sometimes talk about it as though it is easy. 'Forgive and forget,' we say. 'Let bygones be bygones.' But we can't forget something that has devastated us, either in war or in personal circumstances. Forgiveness does not mean letting people off as though what they have done doesn't matter, and it doesn't exclude due punishment. Forgiveness means setting people free. Forgiveness is not forgetting, it's learning to remember differently. It's saying, 'What happened was evil, and it hurt, but I'm not going to let it poison my life any more.' When we can say that, we set ourselves free, too. Forgiveness starts with us being changed. It's not easy or cheap, but it's the way to the life of fullness and peace, the life to which God invites us.

There are many examples of people who have learned the truth of that in their own experience. Eric Lomax is one, and he tells his story in the book *The Railway Man*.[1] He suffered imprisonment and torture while the Burma/Siam Railway was being built, and was left at the end of the war with a terrible anger against those who had tortured him, especially the man who had acted as the interpreter at his interrogations. His story tells how, eventually, Eric came face to face with that man who, like himself, was scarred and haunted by his experience. Eric commented that he realized that there came a point where the hating had to stop.

Being a peacemaker means taking life seriously, facing up to its pain, and helping people set each other free from memories that lock them into hatred. And that's not easy. When Jesus tried living in a spirit of forgiveness, he was crucified, and he carries the scars for eternity. But it's better to have scars than running sores.

So we remember. We remember those killed in war, and those scarred by war, with deep gratitude for the sacrifices they and their families made. The red poppy will always be a symbol of that. And we remember so that we take the lessons of history to heart. A white poppy is worn by a growing number of people as a sign of commitment to justice and peace. Red and white poppies are not alternatives, but complement each other.

And we remember because it's one of the great Bible words, calling us back again and again to God's faithfulness, and his will that his people should live in love. And each time we meet for a Eucharist, we remember Jesus who suffered and was raised to life so that we might have life in all its fullness. Let's open ourselves up to the possibility that life really can be different because we remember.

NOTE

1. Eric Lomax, *The Railway Man*, Vintage Books.

For thine is the kingdom

As the Church's year ends, Ordinary Time slips almost imperceptibly into the Kingdom Season, culminating in the celebration of the festival of Christ the King.

The kingdom of God is what the whole year has been about. But what comes to mind when we hear the words 'king' or 'kingdom'? Perhaps other words like power, wealth, glamour, lands, possessions, banquets – mostly words that are remote from our experience. The British Royal Family has made valiant efforts to be less remote, but we still find it hard to think of the Royals as people like us: it is difficult to think of the Queen queuing at a supermarket checkout, Prince Philip running for a bus, or the royal children eating fish and chips out of newspaper.

In the Kingdom Season, we are asked to celebrate Christ as King, just at the point when the Christian Church is moving towards the celebration of Christmas, when God came to live in the world as one of us. We won't be able to do it if we think about Jesus as a king in the tradition of our historical monarchs. Jesus told us that we need to turn our ideas about kingship upside down, if we are really going to understand how he is King.

The way had been prepared for the new style of kingship by the prophets. Jeremiah, for example, had said (Jeremiah 23.1-6) that the rulers had not looked after their people properly, and so a new king was coming, sent by God, who would really care for his people. And then Jesus came and said to anyone who would listen, 'The time is fulfilled, and the kingdom of God has come near; repent and believe in the good news' (Mark 1.15). The good news was, is, that God is creating something new, turning our ideas round, turning us round. For that is what repentance means, quite simply 'turning round'.

Jesus talked a great deal about the kingdom, and he made it quite clear that God's kingdom is not like the kingdoms that his hearers knew about, where the ruler was all powerful, and the people knuckled under or took the consequences. The king/lord/master in Jesus' stories was not a despot, ordering people around for his own pleasure, but someone who respected what people had to offer and repeatedly gave them opportunities to grow and flourish. All were welcome in his kingdom, except those who oppressed and ill-treated others. For example, the man in one of Jesus' stories who was let off an enormous debt, and then tried to throttle someone who owed him very little got short shrift (Matthew 18.23-35). So did the person who was so jealous of other people's gifts that he refused to use his own, and buried it to keep it safe until he could hand it back to his master undeveloped (Matthew 25.14-30).

God's kingdom is the realization, the making real, of a vision of life where everyone achieves their potential. Jesus worked to establish that kingdom. He challenged people into new ways of thinking; he removed some of the obstacles to people's growth to fullness of life, sometimes by healing physical or mental illness, sometimes by healing spiritual dis-ease by offering acceptance of people as they were, encouraging them to believe that God's love could embrace even them. The dying thief we read about in Luke 23.39-43 was only the last in a long line of people like Zacchaeus, and Peter, lepers and others on the edge of society. Wherever people responded, the kingdom of God began to arrive. The kingdom is very near – but it is not here yet.

There's a lovely little cameo in Mark's Gospel (Mark 12.41-44), where Jesus pointed to a widow who was giving all that she had – not calculating how much of her life she would offer, not even telling others what she was doing, just getting on with offering her life to God. If we all did that, the world would be a very different place. And, of course, we have begun to make that offering – though we know in our hearts that the kingdom of complete response to God is some way off. But the kingdom is coming: it begins to be a reality wherever people adopt the kingdom values of love and justice, forgiveness and living in peace.

When we pray, 'Your kingdom come', it is not only a prayer about what needs to happen in the lives of other people. It is a prayer about what needs to happen in us. That's where it has to start. 'Repent,' said Jesus. Keep turning round to focus on God. That's what Advent will call us to again. May your kingdom come in us, Lord. Transform us, and through us all whom we meet and influence, to your glory.

Copyright Acknowledgements

Section 1:

p. 13   William Temple, 'Christus Veritas' (essay), Macmillan, London, 1924.

p. 21-22   Psalm by Robin Harger written in a workshop at a Parish Weekend.

p. 31   Alan Ecclestone, Article entitled 'Prayer', in *Firing the Clay*, ed. Jim Cotter, Cairns, 1999.

Section 2:

p. 90   W.H. Frere, Prayer, location unknown. Used with permission of Community of the Resurrection, Mirfield.

p. 95   Anthony Bloom, *Courage to Pray*, DLT, 1973, p.15.

p. 98-99   John V. Taylor, *A Matter of Life and Death*, SCM, 1986, p.49. Used with permission of the Estate of John V. Taylor.

p. 127   John A.T. Robinson, Quoting John Hick in *Truth is Two Eyed*, SCM, 1979, p.107.

Section 3:

p. 144   Peruvian Gloria, *A Wee Worship Book*, (fourth incarnation), Wild Goose Worship Group 1999, p.116

p. 160   Henri Nouwen, *Life of the Beloved*, H&S, 1993.

p. 176   Dorothy Frances Gurney, 1858-1932, 'God's Garden'.

p. 189   Simon Bailey, *Stations*, Cairns Publications, 1991.

p. 193   D. T. Niles, *That they may have Life*, Lutterworth, 1952, p.96.

p. 209-210   John V. Taylor, Sanctus (Christmas Card poem 1993), unpublished. Used by permission of the Estate of the late John V. Taylor.

p. 229   Eric Lomax, *The Railway Man*, Vintage Books, 1996.

AROUND
TONBRIDGE
IN OLD PHOTOGRAPHS

'TONBRIDGE, with its grey castle ruins overlooking the winding river, its quaint old Chequers Inn, and the house of the Port Reeve and its famous school, is likely to engage more than the casual interest of the traveller. It is a very pleasant town, intermingling the old and the new in romantic fashion.' (21)

AROUND
TONBRIDGE
IN OLD PHOTOGRAPHS

COLLECTED BY
CHARLIE BELL

ALAN SUTTON

Alan Sutton Publishing Limited
Phoenix Mill · Far Thrupp · Stroud · Gloucestershire

First published 1992

British Library Cataloguing in Publication Data

Around Tonbridge in old photographs.
I. Bell, Charlie, *1952–*
942.237

ISBN 0-86299-892-1

Typeset in 9/10 Korinna.
Typesetting and origination by
Alan Sutton Publishing Limited.
Printed in Great Britain by
The Bath Press, Avon.

CONTENTS

THE MEDWAY ABOVE TONBRIDGE, 1900.

INTRODUCTION

Most of the photographs in this book come from the golden age of black and white photography. Many of the pictures are taken from postcards which, at that time, seemed to regard almost any person, place or event as being worthy subjects for the camera. They are valuable not only because they do this, but also because they give us glimpses into a way of life so different from ours as to be almost alien. People and animals saunter casually on what are now very busy roads, villages bask in a calmness and quietness that seems impossible today and there is not a traffic light, roundabout or white line in sight.

This is not a history book. Rather, it attempts to capture the area as it was over the past hundred and fifty years. I have, as far as is possible, tried to match the pictures to contemporary written accounts. The last quarter of the nineteenth century and the first half of the twentieth were golden years for the guide book as well as for photography, and it seems appropriate to mix the two together in this way. Where interesting local snippets have come my way I have included them.

The administrative area of Tonbridge and Malling is a puzzling entity: the result of a shot-gun wedding in 1974 following local government reforms. Surprisingly, the district stretches northwards almost to Maidstone in the north east and to Sevenoaks in the north west. There are many settlements in this diverse area and I have attempted to represent as many as I can. I could not resist bringing in other places as well, especially to the south of Tonbridge.

The modern reader will perhaps wonder whether, off the motorway, or in the back streets, anything remains of the life style and beauty so often referred to in these pages. If so, I hope that he or she will be stimulated to find out. I have deliberately kept modern comparisons to a minimum so that those who are interested can explore the area for themselves and draw their own conclusions. For those who wish to research things further, there are flourishing historical societies at Tonbridge and West Malling, as well as in some of the villages, but, surprisingly, Tonbridge does not have a museum. The library at Tonbridge contains a wide range of materials to study, as do the County Local Studies centre and the central library at Maidstone.

What emerges from the writings in particular is the sense of pride that the locals had for the area. Kent was truly the Garden of England, dotted with an amazing number of pretty villages and attractive towns set in lush productive countryside. In 1868 Mr R. Ware in *Tonbridge Legends* wrote of Tonbridge: 'The golden hues of an autumn sunset are streaming over the valley of the Wealden and bathing in the myriad hues of an Indian summer a wide district of rare loveliness and unexampled fertility. The silent Medway glides along its bed to the sea, passing under the towers of Tonbridge Castle, robbed of the terror with which feudal cruelty of yore invested them, and clad in ivy that hides while it beautifies decay. The unsightly dwellings of the middle ages have disappeared and streets of modern houses, the homes of highly civilised man, stand in their place. The lagunes of the marshes are gone, for their waters are confined to the channel of the river, and the ruddy orchard and the graceful tendril of the hop now grow along the valley whose low fields once generated the mists that were the exhalations of disease and death.'

A town guide of 1906 asserts: 'Of this we are certain, that when the yearly recurring question, "Where shall I go for my holidays?" is asked, and the respective claims of Devonshire, the Channel Islands, and other localities are canvassed, Tonbridge, but thirty miles from London, can successfully vie with many a popular resort in its recuperative possibilities.

'The locality offers a charming variety of scenery, of hills and valleys, woods, meadows, orchards, hop gardens, and rivers; and presenting ... an unending succession of scenes of natural beauty, Tonbridge only needs to be better known to be the Canaan of thousands who are annually, for a longer or shorter period, liberated from the rigours of business.' (*Tonbridge for the Resident, the Holidaymaker, and the Angler*)

Another guide of 1906 confirms that 'Tonbridge is exceptionally forward in the matter of climate. The town is sheltered by hills on most of its sides, and owing to these high lands thunder-storms are infrequent and wide extremes of temperature are unknown.' (*Mates Illustrated Tonbridge*)

The same source informs us that the death rate for the town was exceptionally low, 'even for this favoured district of Kent,' and gives figures to prove it.

Of Tonbridge itself we have an interesting snapshot of town life in the Town Directory of 1886 in a section listed as 'Local Intelligence'. There were ten churches and chapels; seven schools including the 'Ragged School in Alexandra Road'; a new police station with 'a superintendent, one instructing constable and four other constables'; three Masonic lodges, five temperance associations, and clubs for cricket, boating, angling, skating and cycling. Apart from three building societies, there were three banks: Beeching, Hodgkins & Beeching who drew on

Barclay Bevan & Co., London; London & County Banking Co. and the Savings Bank. There was a gas company at Medway Wharf, and the Tonbridge Water Company. The Tonbridge Free Press proudly served the town, selling at 1d and coming out on Saturdays. In case of emergency, the volunteer steam fire brigade was on call, stationed at the time behind the Rose and Crown Hotel. The Member of Parliament was Robert Norton Esq.

In the rest of the Canaan covered by this book are many villages of interest including West Malling (which thinks of itself as a town). From Maidstone, 'the road to Tonbridge lies through a land or orchards and hops and strawberry fields.' (*Motoring in Kent and Sussex*)

In 1839, in *The Topography of Maidstone*, we find that 'West Malling is situated in and surrounded by most delightful scenery, through which are numerous pleasing walks; the salubrity of this part is not to be excelled in the county.'

From West Malling, the world seems different and Tonbridge a million miles away. One can understand why the locals still feel a sense of identity and separateness despite the workings of the Local Government Reform Act of 1974. The Malling RDC Guide in 1971 boasted that the area of the Rural District was 45,655 acres, covering 71 square miles and including 24 civil parishes.

Running through the district and providing a continuous link is the River Medway, Kent's principal river. As we journey around the area in this book we will keep returning to its graceful and still largely peaceful banks.

The numbers quoted at the end of some captions refer to the sources of quotations printed on p. 159.

SECTION ONE

Tonbridge Town

TONBRIDGE FROM QUARRY HILL in 1896. Despite the poor quality of the photograph there is a pastoral feel to Tonbridge's favourite hill at this time. Note the glasshouse centre right and the spire of St Stephen's church in the centre background. The major development of the Quarry Hill Estate (St Mary's, Springwell Road, Woodfield Road and The Drive) was held back for several years because of planning disputes but work began in 1892. The first dwelling to be occupied was Fairholme, built by Mr William Baldwin who took up residence in September 1892. Work on what is now called the Baltic Estate followed closely. It was called this because it was built on land owned by the partners in the Baltic Sawmills Company.

THE OLD ROAD at the crest of Quarry Hill in Edwardian times. 'The ascent is tedious and long, but the surface is good.' (2)

'QUARRY HILL is the direct and beautiful way to Tunbridge Wells.' (1) 'The road from Tunbridge Wells to Tonbridge is one of the most beautiful in the county, being carried for the whole distance on the ridge of a hill that affords exquisite views on both sides.' (9)

THE VIADUCT OF THE A21 TONBRIDGE BYPASS, completed in the early 1970s. (Norman Rout) The building of the bypass was to change the form and beauty of Quarry Hill forever. In an eloquent piece of prose a reporter for the *Courier* echoed the corporate cry of anguish raised by residents of Tonbridge when he described the building works as follows: 'Lambs Bank looks like a straight case of rape.... Stand on the Cottage Hospital footpath ... and everything has gone – bushes, copses, ponds, the two woods which divided the fields, the mole-hilled slopes of the best tobogganing field for miles around.' (*Courier*, 11 July 1969) The construction caused fundamental change to the whole area including taking away a good deal of the garden of Mabledon, the large house at the very top. The shape of the site was so awkward that it was not possible to include southbound access or northbound exit roads on the A21 at this point.

THE COTTAGE HOSPITAL, built near the top of Quarry Hill, was opened in 1902 to commemorate the reign of Queen Victoria. Its functions were transferred to Vauxhall Lane in 1935. In the 1960s it was well known – and sometimes feared – as the clinic of the school dental service.

'THE DISTRICT CHURCH OF ST STEPHEN at the south end of the town, below the railway, was erected in 1852, and occupies a commanding position at the junction of Quarry Hill and Primrose Hill. The exterior appearance is somewhat pleasing.' (19)

THE BOYS OF ST STEPHEN'S SCHOOL stretching out across Waterloo Road – something which would be unwise today. The postcard was posted in 1913. The buildings at the end on the right no longer exist although modern hackney carriages still queue along the station wall in the middle background. The wall was rebuilt as part of the station refurbishment in the early 1980s.

PEMBURY ROAD, Tonbridge, showing one of the most prominent environmental problems of the time: horse dung in the road. The police station, built in 1864, is on the left nearest the camera.

THE STATION FAÇADE, even as originally built, was no great architectural masterpiece, but it emanated an air of respectable solidity. The railway first reached Tonbridge in 1842, via Redhill, and the first passenger station was on the other side of the bridge in the goods yard. The Sevenoaks connection came in 1868 when the station was moved to its current position. 'The way out of Tonbridge lies . . . past the station, where the banging of trucks and the screaming of whistles are continuous, and South Eastern trains are, like practical jokers, for ever pretending to be going off, just to flurry and excite nervous passengers, and then coming back and casually shunting up and down the sidings when they ought to be miles away.' (34)

THE FAÇADE was later altered and lasted until the 1980s when it was given its current tiled facing, thus attracting the criticism that it looks like a public lavatory. At the time of this 1960s photograph, the space inside the entrance doors to the right housed a W.H. Smith news kiosk.

TONBRIDGE STATION in the early 1960s, looking south on platform 1.

LOOKING NORTH from platform 2 we can clearly see the old signal box and signal gantry. Indications that we are still in the age of steam are the water fillers on either side of the platform.

LOOKING NORTH AGAIN we can see, centre right, the T. Ives cricket factory, part of the specialized industry which made Tonbridge famous.

A STEAM TRAIN SITS AT THE PLATFORM but the days of steam are numbered as can be seen by the electric rail on the main line (foreground). The Sevenoaks–Tonbridge–Dover section of the Kent Coast electrification programme was completed in 1962. When steam trains were withdrawn on the Tonbridge–Hastings line, special narrow diesel units were supplied to cope with the narrow tunnels. These were the result of poor workmanship on the line which meant that the tunnels had to be lined with extra layers of brick. Electrification of this line was completed in 1986.

LOOKING SOUTH. The column left centre is for filling the engines with water. A sign on the reverse warns enginemen that 'Due to high pressure of water at this column care must be exercised to avoid spillage.'

THE RAILWAY DISASTER AT TONBRIDGE, 5 March 1909. The accident occurred when the Charing Cross to Dover Boat Train struck a local train which had ignored stop signals. Two railway workers were killed. The tragedy struck only forty minutes before the Royal Train was scheduled to pass through.

THE ANGEL CRICKET GROUND, Tonbridge, now the site of Sainsburys, Bentalls department store, the Angel Leisure Centre and large car parks.

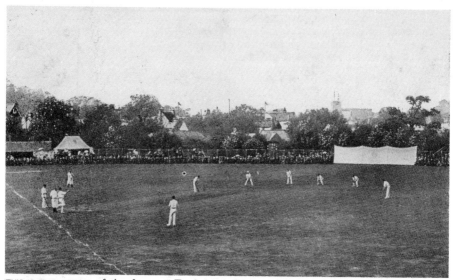

THIS IS THE SCENE of the famous Tonbridge Cricket Festival (usually held in June). No account of Tonbridge would be complete without reference to Cricket, and Tonbridge School and Tonbridge Town have been prominent in support of the game so pre-eminently Kentish. Players like Rashleigh, the Wilsons, Leslie and Cecil, the le Flemings, Hutchins and Wright have emerged from the academic nursery, whilst Blythe, Fielder, Seymour, Hardinge, Woolley and Humphreys have been produced by that excellent nursery for Kent professional cricketers established at Tonbridge. . . . With such surroundings a Cricket Week was inevitable.' (29)

ANGEL CORNER, TONBRIDGE. The Angel Hotel is on the right and was demolished in 1972 after being damaged by the floods of 1968. In an advert of 1911, the Angel offered a livery and bait stables along with a garage and billiards room.

BEHIND THE ANGEL, to the right of our picture, lay the Tonbridge cricket ground. To the left is the Technical Institute and Free Library, built in 1900 for £7,000 and now the Library and Adult Education Centre. The photograph is taken from the area of road which used to exist in front of the station yard and which served as the town's Speaker's Corner and general market place before the Second World War. This useful space vanished during the road improvement of 1968.

PARRY & EDE'S SHOP at No. 77 High Street. In their advert of 1896, they sold nuts, oranges, grapes, figs and dates, and were agents for 'Barrett & Co's celebrated confectionery'. They sold 'all the latest novelties in fancy confectionery'.

THE HIGH STREET before road widening of 1888, showing the old Castle Inn. Note the sign for the Medway Navigation Company, the town's main employer in the nineteenth century. The company was influential in setting up the town's first horse-drawn fire brigade. Note also the gas light on the left. The town's streets were first lit by gas in 1836, the first lanterns being in the High Street, East Street and Bordyke.

THE RECONSTRUCTED GREAT BRIDGE, showing the new Castle Hotel. Buildings on the opposite side of the road were not touched. The widening, although very welcome, contributed to the loss of some of the charm of the old town.

A VIEW FROM SLIGHTLY HIGHER UP THE HIGH STREET, looking back to the Great Bridge and Castle Hotel. On the left is one of the ornate street lamps which once graced the town.

TANK DAY, 29 July 1919. The tank, presented by the War Savings Committee, was finally mounted on the north side of the castle gatehouse.

The Terrace, Tonbridge Castle

'THE GATEWAY IS PERFECT, and the inclosure formed into a vineyard by a Mr Hooker, to whom it belongs, and the walls spread with fruit, and the mount on which the keep stood planted in the same way. The prospect is charming, and the breach in the wall opens to a pretty Gothic bridge of three arches.' (Horace Walpole) Thomas Hooker had the house built in the eighteenth century after failing to convert the towers as a residence. It was regarded as 'a species of architectural sacrilege' at the time and appears an odd juxtaposition even today. The house was built from the remains of the keep and was 'the headquarters of all municipal activity, under the direction of the energetic Urban District Council, whose offices are established there'. (18)

'WHERE THE MAILED BARONS OF THE MIDDLE AGES held stern rule, and governed a race of serfs with a rod of iron, there is now a pile of ruins, which, in other days, was a proud and strong castle. Amidst its ivy-clad and picturesque walls, at whose feet still flows the gentle and silent Medway, is a modern mansion, which is now a seminary of the highest class.' (28)

23

THE GREAT BRIDGE from the Maidstone side. The building nearest the bridge on the right was at this time the post office, and next to it was the Kent Cricket Co. The building displaying the Hovis sign was Beardswells the bakers and next door to that, out of picture, was Wightwicks Corn Merchants, later to become Charlton's and then Cramphorns. It is now a Beefeater restaurant.

FROM THE PENSHURST SIDE we can clearly see the old post office, now a bank, straight ahead. On the left bank of the river was the old Horse-wash, where people would water their horses and clean their carts. Eventually this was filled in to make a new entrance to the Castle Grounds off the High Street.

THE GREAT BRIDGE FROM THE RIVER WALK and the site of the old Horse-wash. The 'Wash' was a bay in the Medway, about thirty to forty feet across. Occasionally it provided a source of much wonder and entertainment when a visiting circus would water and wash its exotic animals, much to the delight of the local children. It was the scene of the drowning of Joseph Featherstone, master baker, in December 1816. He had just entered the Wash to water his horse after delivering bread. Inexplicably he fell from the horse and was washed away by the swiftly flowing current, the river being in flood at the time. The accident was witnessed by a large crowd who watched, horrified but helpless. The tragedy remained in the collective memory of the town for a very long time.

LOOKING TOWARDS THE GREAT BRIDGE from what used to be the Boating Club. 'We will now take a boat from the Castle Hotel and introduce you to the drowsy Medway. After being pulled through the town bridge we see (presumably we are in stern sheets with somebody else doing all the work) on the right the luxuriant gardens and trees of Tonbridge Castle, with a bit of old wall peeping out now and then; on the left the rustic woodwork of the garden of Bartram's Brewery. Ahead is the boathouse of the Tonbridge Boat Club, one of the most beautifully situated clubhouses in the kingdom. The river now winds along between well-wooded banks, the bushes bright in the proper seasons with May blossom, wild roses, alder and dogwood.' (1)

BOATING AT BARDEN PARK. In 1923 the former racecourse was purchased from Mr William Abrey and turned into a large sports ground.

BARDEN PARK HOUSE AND GROUNDS were also purchased from Mr Abrey, who continued to live in the town and do good works. The house was demolished after the Second World War.

THE ENTRANCE TO BARDEN PARK. 'Barden Road was then (1896) a country lane serving Barden Park and House, bounded by hop gardens, oasthouses and other rural features.' (33) The first part of the housing development in this area came in 1895.

THE LANDING STAGE AT BARDEN PARK.

A BAZAAR IN THE GROUNDS OF BARDEN PARK, C. 1904.

SWINGS AND DONKEYS at the Pleasure Grounds, Barden Park.

Above: THE MEDWAY AT SKATING TIME, 1906.

Opposite: 'THAT CALM AND FLOWER FRINGED STREAM.' (18) 'Placid in its beauty as it ever is, it is yet various from its childhood above Edenbridge, and its tree-shadowed stillness under the oaks of Penshurst, to the cowslip-strewn meadows above Yalding, whence we come to the wider opening at Wateringbury and the fairer reaches of Aylesford.' (18) 'Boating is practicable for about two miles above the town and further in a canoe. Downwards, one may row in about 16 miles to Maidstone for the trouble of opening the locks. The tow path (soon) leads into meadows after Izaak Walton's heart.' (6)

'IN DUE COURSE I CAME INTO TONBRIDGE TOWN and, following the High Street, presently observed a fine inn upon the right-hand side of the way, which ... is called the Chequers. And here were divers loiterers, lounging round the door, or seated upon the benches.' (35) 'On entering the inn, one is sadly disappointed to see that the ancient and charming character, which is given the inn by its exterior and for which it is so justly noted, is not borne out by the interior. It is now merely a drinking inn of the alehouse type, but the ancient beams are still there, although covered with match-boarding and plaster.' (30)

THE HIGH STREET in the 1920s, showing the shop of Caleb Moore, family grocer, the Carlton Café, and Gunner's family drapers all on the left hand side. The Carlton was a Tonbridge institution, as was Gunners, whose department store lasted on the same site until the early 1980s. Note Hoad's furniture store at No. 126. On its left was R.W. Dance's saddlers shop. Mr Dance's father was the town's first police superintendent.

LOOKING NORTH FROM THE CHEQUERS in Edwardian times. At the road junction, in front of the piano and organ advertisement and in the road itelf, is the site of the old town hall which 'stood for over 1,000 years when it was acquired by the town. By no means a picturesque building, it formed a considerable obstruction to traffic and was improved off the face of the earth in 1901.' (19)

JOHN ANGELL'S SHOP at Nos 110–112 High Street, a few doors down from the Chequers. The firm still exists, further down the High Street. The original building was demolished in 1962.

Golden Wedding.

September 8th. 1858—1908.

" Ye shall hallow the fiftieth year."

LEV. XXV. 10.

With the

Rev. C. G. & Mrs. Baskerville's Best Wishes

Tonbridge Vicarage.

1908.

THE SOBER CELEBRATION CARD of the Revd C.G. Baskerville and his wife. The church pictured is the parish church of St Peter and St Paul, dating from the twelfth century.

G. & C. J. ROAKE

For Reliable Drapery AT POPULAR PRICES.

Mantles, Jackets, Dresses, Millinery.

Noted for
the Best Makes in
HOSIERY
and
GLOVES.

C.B. and other
Celebrated Makes in
CORSETS.

Horrockses'
CALICOES and
SHEETINGS.

FLANNELS,
BLANKETS,
and
HOUSEHOLD
LINENS
in the Best Makes.

CURTAINS, CARPETS, **WINDOW BLINDS** made and fitted to order.
FLOORCLOTHS, RUGS. **UPHOLSTERY WORK** of all kinds undertaken

ESTIMATES FREE. **126 HIGH STREET, TONBRIDGE.**

THIS ADVERTISEMENT of 1906 was taken before the renumbering of the High Street in the early 1900s. The building still stands and is now numbered 134.

KIMMINS THE CONFECTIONER at what was then No. 135 High Street. An advertisement of 1896 proudly proclaims, 'By appointment to Tonbridge School'. The speciality of the shop was 'The old English loaf, made from the best English flour and mixed entirely with milk – the most nourishing and wholesome bread to be obtained.'

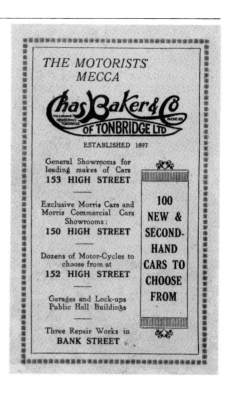

CHAS BAKER & CO. was a leading garage of the time. In an advertisement of 1911 they claimed to be 'leading car agents and official repairers. Agents for Vauxhall, Hotchkiss, Singer, Fiat, Delage and Humber &c.' They also stocked cycles and repaired motorcycles. At that time they had premises at both 150 and 187 High Street. The advertisement and photograph date from the 1920s.

A CHAS BAKER & CO. LTD BOOKLET of motor runs round Tonbridge declared in the 1920s: 'The firm are agents for some of the leading makes of Cars, including Daimler, Wolseley, Humber, Armstrong Siddeley, etc, and a representative range of models are on show at the General Showrooms, whilst a full range consisting of 20 to 30 different models of all the various Morris productions in several colours are shown at their exclusive Morris Show-rooms at 150 High Street.' (36) The firm was incorporated by Caffyns Ltd in 1935. Given Tonbridge's current traffic congestion, it seems ironic that in 1896 the Urban District Council unanimously passed a motion which declared: 'That this Council records its great regret that the present state of the law places needless restrictions on the use of horseless carriages on the public highways and expresses the urgent hope that an amending Act may shortly be placed on the Statute Book.' This hope was fulfilled and the law was changed in the same year.

THE HIGH STREET FROM CHAS BAKER'S. Note the 1920s petrol pump, probably the first public pump in Tonbridge.

A FINE POSE FROM THE MILITARY at the back of Chas Baker's, opposite the fire station.

THE GRAND PARADE of 22 June 1911, celebrating the coronation of King George V. The man leading the first set of horses, which were owned by Lord Hollanden of Leigh, is Mr H.G. Boakes.

THIS MISSIONARY EXHIBITION, entitled 'Africa and the East', was held on 22–30 November 1911 in the room above the Public Hall. There were more exhibits in the Drill Hall behind. The message on the card says: 'You will see me on the left, just in the photo, opposite to the North India Court where I give "talks" two or three times a day, and show the curiosities. WJC'

THE PORT REEVE'S HOUSE. 'Another ancient building of the domestic type is seen on the south side of East Street nearly opposite the vicarage. It is the house of the old fiscal officer who was responsible for levying a toll on all cattle and sheep, and on various other commodities, that entered the town by Postern Gate.' (19) 'This picturesque old landmark was formerly the house of the Port Reeve.... The building is known to be over 450 years old, and an examination of its oaken beams shows it to be as good as ever, and perchance it may yet last for many years. It now consists of three cottages, the building facing the road being once known as the Swan Inn. The diminutive character of its doorways cause the reflection that, although "our fathers were high-minded men", they must have been exceedingly low of stature. Silk hats beware!' (1)

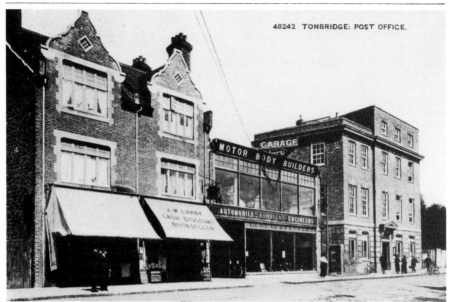

THE NEW POST OFFICE, established during the First World War after moving from the Great Bridge. In 1886 the post office was open from 7 a.m. to 9 a.m. on weekdays, but only from 7 to 10 a.m. on Sundays. There were three deliveries a day but only one on Sunday. The garage to the left was owned by H.E. Hall & Co. who claimed to be 'the sole county agent for the noiseless Napier cars', as well as for Talbots.

A WORKING PARTY READY FOR ACTION. In the early part of the twentieth century the town seems to have been full of troops. These shops, at the north end of the town, are now all gone to help with the road widening.

THE PUBLIC HALL, on the right, was opened in 1873 and was originally used for such things as theatrical performances and concerts, before becoming the Public Hall Kinema in 1921. It closed after a fire on Boxing Day 1926 and reopened as the Capitol Cinema in 1928. Forty years later it was closed again and became a bingo hall, the fate of many a cinema.

THE FIRE BRIGADE, totally unencumbered by the frustrations of modern traffic, has a free run as it heads north on business, passing the Public Hall on the right and Tonbridge Free Press Printing Office on the left. It is thought by some that the crew are on the way to a wedding.

'RETRACING YOUR STEPS to where the school stretches its fair length of buildings, and turfed quadrangle by the roadside, and lingering under the line of clipped elms opposite, shadowed by the high wall they screen, you realise the old town has seen the continuous stream of history flow past to Dover or Hastings or Canterbury and London for many centuries.' (29)

'SO TONBRIDGE SCHOOL HAS COME by grace of time to inherit a quality which is more precious than its present showing, as an old trinket is enhanced by its association and made priceless by a beloved memory.' (18)

TUCK SHOP AND AVENUE, TONBRIDGE SCHOOL. 'On weekdays various coloured caps or ribbons on straw hats mark the "houses" to which the wearers belong, while the general black and white straw merges all the houses in uniform for Sunday.' (8)

TONBRIDGE SCHOOL, SKINNERS DAY ANNUAL INSPECTION, 1915. 'The first event on Skinners Day is the bathing. All the boys except the juniors go down to the bathing place about seven o'clock in the morning, and on a given signal all jump into the water together, and after the bathing is over go round in a body to the various masters' houses and cheer lustily for a minute or two each. The custom appears to date from a period when washing was less common than it is at present.' (1)

THE STAR AND GARTER on the corner of London Road and Shipbourne Road at the turn of the twentieth century.

DRY HILL, SHIPBOURNE ROAD, Tonbridge, looking back to the Star and Garter. On the left is Mathers, the greengrocers. The building was demolished in the 1930s.

DRY HILL, TONBRIDGE, at the rear of the Star and Garter on the Shipbourne Road. 'A picturesque group of cottages suffered the swifter and more terrible foe – fire – some few years ago but the repairs have been affected with admirable skill and discretion.' (29) The fire occurred at Featherstone's baker on 14 March 1903. It 'destroyed the symmetry of the picture, and the new bakery and adjoining boot-maker's shop, while more roomy and convenient, do not entirely harmonise with the row of cottages on Dry Hill Bank.' (33)

DERNIER ROAD, TONBRIDGE, after a British bomber had crashed, without bombs on board, on 26 October 1940. Three people died.

TONBRIDGE COUNTY SCHOOL, DEAKIN LEAS, now the Grammar School for Girls, moved to this site in 1913.

THE WORKSHOP AT JUDD SCHOOL, Brook Street, Tonbridge, 1932. The boy front centre holding the saw became Squadron Leader Neville Duke DSO, AFC, DFC, and 2 Bars, whose father ran Charlton's the Corn Chandlers. Behind him to the right is Squadron Leader D.R. Fisher DFC, DFM, who was killed in action. On the other side of the bench is Wing Commander A.E. Millson DSO, DFC and Bar.

AFTER THE DECLARING OF THE POLL at the Castle in January 1910 a large crowd gathered outside the Rose and Crown to hear the successful candidate, Capt. Spender Clay (Cons).

FROM THE COUNCIL OFFICES ADJOINING THE CASTLE the Returning Officer declares the result of a second Parliamentary election held in December of the same year. Spender Clay was once again successful.

CAPTAIN SPENDER CLAY (centre), Conservative Member of Parliament, leaving the parish church.

TWO OF THE WICKENDEN FAMILY of No. 8 Danvers Road, taken between the two world wars. The street is empty of parked cars and children could presumably play in the streets in relative safety.

TONBRIDGE can claim an early involvement with motor cars. In 1835 a steam carriage owned by Messrs Ogle and Summers of London spent a week in the town giving excursions. Mr Alfred Cornell, a Tonbridge jeweller, owned the first Mercedes in Tonbridge and drove it, in defiance of the law, without the red flag until eventually brought to book and fined. The picture, taken around 1896, is probably of Mr Cornell. Three miles away in Southborough lived Sir David Salomons, who pioneered the first British motor show at Tunbridge Wells.

Next page: MRS G. BAKER outside her house at No. 11 Baltic Road, Tonbridge during the Second World War. (*Kent Messenger*) The Kent WVS undertook garment mending on a large and small scale. In Maidstone Borough and Maidstone Rural areas, in the three months from April to June 1943, they mended 67,991 garments! Tonbridge had its own WVS centre which, on one occasion, managed to sew 2,884 flashes onto uniforms overnight ready for a battalion inspection! The centre's work was supplemented by Mrs Baker's 'Mend while you wait' service for soldiers, which was apparently very popular.

MEND WHILE
YOU WAIT

AN IMPRESSIVE DISPLAY at a flower and produce show in the town, held at the beginning of the twentieth century.

THE PEOPLE OF TONBRIDGE LIKED THEIR CELEBRATIONS. This one is probably Coronation Day in 1911. One of the town's special events, Commemoration Day, was held every year, on the Wednesday nearest 24 May. It was a general holiday to celebrate both Queen Victoria's birthday and the acquisition by the town of the Castle Grounds. About 2,500 children marched in procession to the Castle and enjoyed themselves at various attractions throughout the afternoon. After the children had left, by the Slade gate, the public were admitted at a small charge. The custom ended at the beginning of the First World War. This seems a shame for 'Tonbridge folk came nearer in these days to a revival of "Merrie England" than had been seen hereabouts since the days of Good Queen Bess.' (33)

A NUMBER OF CAMPS WERE HELD AT TONBRIDGE prior to the First World War, one of which was the annual camp of the East Kent Yeomanry at Somerhill.

THE CITY OF LONDON ROYAL FUSILIERS relaxing during the First World War. The picture would have been suitable for an early 'Spot the Ball' competition.

LORD FRENCH awarding the Military Medal for bravery in the field to Private Laverack of the Somerset Light Infantry on 29 June 1917. The occasion was an inspection of the Officer Training Corps and took place on Martin's Field. Other postcards of the event depict the March Past and Lord French addressing the men.

TONBRIDGE SALVATION ARMY BAND, c. 1905. The band is notable for its wide range of ages, from the splendid walrus-mustachioed gentleman at the centre rear to the young drummer boy in the front row.

THE PRODUCTION OF CRICKETING EQUIPMENT has long made the town famous. Cricket ball manufacture is one of Tonbridge's oldest industries, a descendant of the saddle makers' craft. Tonbridge water was apparently particularly suitable for tanning the leather. Cricket lovers will recognize the famous names of Duke & Son, Stuart Surridge, John Wisden, Gray Nicholls and Twort & Sons who eventually amalgamated into Tonbridge Sports Industries. Above: A skilled craftsman sews the two halves of leather around a cricket ball which consists of a cork middle wound with twine. He is making tiny stitches using special waxed thread. Each person made up his own thread and covers and each had his own preferred wax for polishing. At one time all Test Match and most County balls came from Tonbridge and, in the 1960s, twenty-three craftsmen made 30,000 balls a year. The great days of hand-made cricket manufacture in the town are now over, with only a small factory remaining in the area. The pictures were taken in the 1950s. (*Kent Messenger*)

Opposite: Which famous player got to use this bat?

AN UNDATED PHOTOGRAPH OF A CHEERY FLOWER GIRL in Tonbridge. (*Kent Messenger*) Tonbridge was not short of interesting plants and flowers. 'The valley of the Medway and the fields and hedgerows in its immediate vicinity form a veritable Tom Tiddler's Ground for the botanist. So favourable are the conditions for plant life, and so varied the soil, that one finds not only a wide range of species, but for the most part, luxuriant growth and bountiful blossom.' (1)

THE GENERATING ROOM OF TONBRIDGE POWER STATION at The Slade in the 1930s. (Seeboard)

MR E. RHODES, POWER STATION ATTENDANT, around 1945. (Seeboard) The power station was built in 1902, its consulting engineer being Robert Hammond, one of the leading promoters of electricity at the time. An early attempt at a combined heat and power operation led to the open-air swimming pool being heated by surplus heat from the power station, a scheme commissioned in 1910. Power generation at The Slade ceased in the 1950s and the building became the Milne Electricity Museum, which is now also closed pending a move to the Chalkpits Museum at Amberley, West Sussex.

THE ORIGINAL 1902 SWITCHBOARD. (Seeboard) Generation began in 1902 and was three wire direct current at 220–440 volts. In 1916 electricity was being supplied at 6d per unit. Sir Humphrey Davy was a frequent visitor to Ferox Hall in Tonbridge, developing battery technology with Mr John George Children in the nineteenth century. The two scientists were also partners with the Burtons of Mabledon, in the Leigh Powder Mills. Two other early electrical pioneers who later lived close by were Sir David Salmons at Southborough and Sir William Siemens at Tunbridge Wells.

THE INTERIOR OF THE MILNE MUSEUM BEFORE CLOSURE. The large pillar box at the back is a cast iron transformer kiosk dating from 1910. (RCHME)

THE POWER STATION CHIMNEY BEING DISMANTLED at the start of the Second World War to avoid it being a landmark for German pilots. The chimney had been disused for some time previously. (Seeboard)

FOUR WORKERS of the Tonbridge UDC Electricity Department posing for the camera in 1936. They are from left to right: Dick Luckhurst, Guy Horn, Frank Cheal (?) and Charlie Channing. Mr Channing's car is a 1927 Austin 'Chummy' tourer. (Seeboard)

OVERHEAD LINESMEN erecting an overhead EHT (Extra High Tension) power line at Tudeley in 1939. (Seeboard)

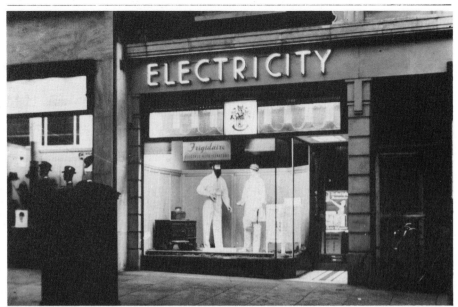

TONBRIDGE URBAN DISTRICT COUNCIL ELECTRICITY SHOP WINDOW in 1939, presumably during Cricket Week. (Seeboard)

A SELECTION OF APPLIANCES available from the Tonbridge Electricity Shop. (Seeboard) This picture was taken in 1936. In 1947, an advertisement for the shop at No. 111 High Street promised 'an all-electric home equipped with electric cooker, water heater, wash boiler, refrigerator, etc. will prove more economical and give you more leisure, greater comfort, better health'.

AN EARLY PICTURE of the resplendently bearded Tonbridge Police Division, which at one time covered eighteen parishes. (Kent County Constabulary) Before the police station was built in Pembury Road, the prisoners had to be locked in two 'cages', one in Bank Street and the other in Barden Road. 'They are remembered by a few venerable residents as small square buildings of red brick, whose substantial oak doors were generously studded with iron nails and whose square iron gratings not only admitted light and air, but facilitated the supply of refreshment to those within.' (33)

TONBRIDGE FIRE BRIGADE VOLUNTEERS in their depot in the Rose and Crown Yard before their move to new premises in Bank Street in 1901. (Kent Fire Brigade) They are showing off their equipment, which included a steam pump, manual pump and fire escape, all manufactured by Shan Mason & Co. They also boasted 500 yd of hose.

THE OLD TONBRIDGE FIRE STATION in Bank Street, built in 1901 for £1,800, 'a very satisfactory building providing accommodation for the fire engines, fire escape and other appliances, and also – queer combination – a room serving the purposes of a court for the local coroner.' (19) (Kent Fire Brigade)

FIREMEN POSING WITH THEIR PERSONNEL CARRIER at what appears to be an open day or official function. (Kent Fire Brigade)

PRINCE ARTHUR ON INSPECTION at the Fire Brigades Week. The Tonbridge brigade was highly regarded nationally and was honoured by the holding of a national Fire Brigades Week in 1909.

'THE TONBRIDGE FIRE BRIGADE is an up-to-date body of men, who, by their prowess in national competitions and by their general smartness, have earned the admiration of their contemporaries.' (19)

TONBRIDGE HAS SUFFERED GREATLY from flood damage over the years. The last major catastrophe occurred in 1968. Left is the scene outside Gunners Department Store. (Norman Rout)

THE GREAT BRIDGE being traversed by an army amphibious vehicle and a tractor in 1968. (Norman Rout)

A DRAMATIC VIEW OF THE 1968 FLOODS AT NIGHT, looking south down the High Street from the corner of Medway Wharf Road. (Norman Rout)

CANNON BRIDGE AFTER THE FLOODS of 1968. Note the high voltage electricity cable still intact. (Seeboard)

A FLOOD BARRIER was erected on the River Medway above Tonbridge after the 1968 floods. (Norman Rout)

THE LOW PROFILE MECHANISM uses radial sluices to control the water. When the barrier is in use the flood water backs right up to Penshurst. (Norman Rout)

SECTION TWO

A Trip Around the Borough

'NORTH OF TONBRIDGE, on the road to Sevenoaks, is the quiet village of Hildenborough, famous on many cricketing fields as a place where some of the best bats and balls are made.' (26)

7835. Cemetery for Dogs & Cats. "The Boiling Kettle", Hildenborough.

THE PET CEMETERY AT THE BOILING KETTLE CAFÉ, Hildenborough, on the corner of Hilden Park Road, now the site of a filling station. The inscriptions have an amusing turn of phrase.

Opposite page: THE OLD BARN TEAROOMS, between Hildenborough and Leigh. 'Our first customers were members of a cinema company, who were making a picture in Penshurst. Driving up one day in three Daimler cars, they demanded a farmhouse tea and refused to leave without it. Out came our cream, butter, and eggs, and loud were the praises of our farmhouse fare.... The simple fact that a new laid egg on the farm was worth one penny, but when boiled fetched fourpence, decided me to start the teahouse business.' (27) The astute and eccentric Commander Tomlinson made a very prosperous business from these beginnings. In its heyday the teahouse boasted a swimming pool, lake and paddle boats, a menagerie, and a working flour mill, along with a host of other enticements. At one time there was even an airfield. People came from many miles around, including London. On a Sunday afternoon in the 1920s and '30s it was not unusual to serve 2,000 teas. Its huge ballroom was famous for its Saturday night dances. The trademark of the establishment was 'Oceans of Cream'.

6373. The Ballroom, Old Barn Teahouse, Hildenborough.

UNFORTUNATELY, THE TEAROOMS CLOSED in 1990 after seventy years. In 1991 the complex was still for sale, with the asking price being over £1,000,000.

'IN THE PAST FEW YEARS . . . Hildenborough has won something of a new celebrity, for here for several winters village players have performed specially written dramatic pieces. The project was first devised about five years ago to afford winter evenings' amusement for the men of the village and many of them proved apt actors in the little plays of old Kentish life written for them by Mr Dagney Major. . . . I have heard it referred to as an extremely interesting experiment in training the minds of the men and boys who are members of the village institute and giving them employment on winter evenings. It has done all this and much more. It has shown that men can be easily drawn from the inanities of the taproom, and that even in a little community like this there exists a strong natural talent for reproducing the drama of life.' (26)

'NINE MILES FROM TONBRIDGE is the exceedingly pretty village of Shipbourne.... The houses are built mostly round an extensive green, and the whole has an air of comfort and respectability that naturally creates a feeling of interest in the place.' (12) 'We come out into the green land again at Shipbourne, a place of rhododendrons.' (20)

THE WEST KENT HUNT meeting outside the Chaser pub at Shipbourne in the 1950s. The village was home to the poet Christopher Smart. (*Kent Messenger*)

THE PLAXTOL OF THE EARLY TWENTIETH CENTURY. 'It is one of the charming little places up and down the hills round Sevenoaks, a secluded corner of Kent just off its main roads.' (5)

PLAXTOL appears to mean 'play place', a piece of land set aside for sport and recreation. Its Old English origin has connections with the name Plaistow near Bromley.

'PLAXTOL is rich in old houses. We found a happy company of craftsmen working at the old fifteenth-century forge much as men worked in medieval days, singing as they made beautiful gates, splendid door handles, and a solid copper model of the Golden Hind to sail high above the Darent Valley.' (5)

THIS PHOTOGRAPH, taken in the 1950s, shows the old forge in the left foreground. It was still working as a forge in 1953.

PLAXTOL SCHOOLS in 1920. They were built in 1847 and later became the Plaxtol and Shipbourne Memorial Hall.

PLAXTOL MIXED GROUP 3 some time during the first decade of the twentieth century.

'I climbed up to the genial shelter of the Kentish Rifleman inn at Dunks Green, where the landlord produced some home-made brawn and cheese sandwiches and the ancients discussed all the footpaths they knew for miles around.' (10)

CHURCH ROAD, PLATT, looking towards Borough Green, depicted on a postcard sent in 1920.

IGHTHAM VILLAGE in Edwardian times. To the left is Town House (1480) and the Commercial Hotel, later to become the George and Dragon. On the right is the Railway Bell, destined to become Arthur's Garage and now converted to housing. 'The Town House is an ancient and lovely building of vertical timber, and as I turned right-handed past the front of it I came next door to an equally old and equally picturesque building, the fifteenth-century George and Dragon Inn with low-beamed ceilings, and an atmosphere about it of comfort and good taste.' (10)

REMEMBRANCE DAY AT IGHTHAM in the 1950s. The George and Dragon (1515) and the Garage (1515). (*Kent Messenger*)

'IGHTHAM, anciently written Eightham, and so called. . . . from its comprising eight Boroughs or Hams, is a village of moderate extent through which runs the high road to Maidstone.' (14)

IGHTHAM in the days when villages were still served by a variety of shops. This 1950s photograph shows W.H. Sherman, newsagents and general stores, and, beyond it, Gilbert Smith the grocers, displaying the ubiquitous Hovis sign.

A ROCK SHELTER ON OLDBURY HILL, Ightham. There appears to have been settlement here from prehistoric through to Roman times. (*Kent Messenger*) 'Near the rough steps leading up to the camp on the Eastern side, about two hunded years ago, a murder was committed here and the murderer was duly hanged in chains on a gibbet close by the scene of the crime. The place was long known as Gibbet or Gallows Field, and when the neighbouring mill was burnt down two or three years ago, the iron cage in which the murderer's body had been hung was unearthed.' (26)

THE SMALL VILLAGE OF HADLOW, like many of its contemporaries, showed a wide diversity of economic activity in the later part of the nineteenth century. It had two breweries, several brickfields, a gas works, a coffee tavern, a fizzy drink manufacturer, fifteen farmers, a plant nursery and over thirty other occupations.

HADLOW. 'In a park which has some fine cedar trees is a queer house called The Castle, with a tall pinnacled tower, a well known landmark in Central Kent.' (7) 'There is a house belonging to Mr May, the most singular thing I ever saw. An immense house stuck all over with a parcel of chimneys, or things like chimneys, little brick columns, with a sort of cap on them.' (25)

SOPHIA RODGER OF HADLOW CASTLE. When she died in 1887 she left a will remarkable for the amount of jewellery and other valuables gave away. Even the housekeeper and the wife of the coachman received generous gifts of clothing and time pieces. Sophia also left £300 to be invested to provide a Christmas dinner for the oldest fifty members of the parish. This custom, which lasted many years, has been overtaken by inflation. Now the money is aggregated with two other charities and given in cash every few years.

HADLOW BOY SCOUTS about 1910. Back row: Joe Marsh, Fred Restall, P. Mankelow, Leslie Wilmshurst, -?-, -?-, Stanley Norville, Frank Norville. Middle row (seated): Fred Manser, Fred Pullen, Percy Burr (scoutmaster), -?-, Harold Hailstone (did layouts for *Punch*; his younger brother Bernard became a famous portrait painter). Front row: Jimmy Owen, Eric Hailstone, ? Manser, ? Skinner. Five generations of the Manser family worked for the brewery.

AN UNDATED BUT FINE PICTURE of the Stone Family at Four Wents near Hadlow. The building was apparently destroyed during the Second World War.

THIS FARMAN GOLIATH AIRLINER, run by the Languedoc Company, came down on Three Elm Lane near Hadlow in August 1924. Only slight injuries were sustained by passengers and crew. The plane is being guarded by PC Ernest Wells.

THE COCKPIT appears to have been open to the elements and the machine looks far too ungainly to fly. In fact, one of the engines had failed and the pilot, Captain P.C.M. Delesle, had tried to put down in a large field.

'SET IN A VERY PICTURESQUE COUNTRY of hilly parklands and woods, Mereworth is regarded as one of the show places to be visited either from Maidstone or Tonbridge.' (26) Mereworth was, at one time, at the centre of a major hop growing area. Every year, there would be an invasion of hop pickers from London. 'Whey they had dragged their way up from the railway station, halting at every pub on the road, the invaders swarmed over (us) like ants, arrogant as conquerors, erasing the village's quiet and orderly habits out of existence, like a wet sponge over the neat writing of a child's slate. . . . Once the strangers had settled themselves in their huts and tents, they took complete possession of (the place). They were respecters of neither persons nor things. If there was fruit it stood to reason that the fruit was for eating: if there were fields it stood to reason they were for everybody's use, when and how they pleased; and so they roamed about at will, breaking branches off trees, soiling everywhere, and scattering their refuse all over the countryside. The local policeman was quite unable to do anything about it.' (37)

'THE VIEW FROM WROTHAM HILL across the valley of the Medway is of astonishing effect. Far-off miles and miles away the hills continue their interminable line, until lost in that grey-blue that fades at last into a mere sky upon the extreme east.' (23) 'Perhaps it never presented a more charming aspect than in those days of August 1894, when the rich hues of harvest time combined with the fresh green of foliage due to the long, wet summer. As far as the eye could reach, over hill and dale stretched the squares of crimson, red, gold, vivid yellow . . . and here and there darker grey patches of the long grass, for haymaking had scarcely commenced although the corn was fast ripening.' (15) (*Kent Messenger*)

'THE HIGH ROAD, as it is in every sense, rises to over 700 ft, then drops, by a descent, ill-famed among cyclists, to Wrotham, pronounced Rootam.' (6)

BUTTS HILL, WROTHAM. Just out of picture there was a sign, existing until recent times, exhorting those in charge of horses to 'Slacken your reins when going up the hill.'

WROTHAM. 'At the foot of the chalk hills. A very ancient town. The "Broteham" of the Domesday Book.' (2) 'Wrotham is an exceptionally attractive village of old red brick houses, all of them roofed with red tiles.' (10) These two views of Wrotham High Street show the same part from two opposing viewpoints. The Rose and Crown is on the left in the top picture and on the right at the bottom; vice versa for the George and Dragon. The shop on the corner (top picture) appears to be very versatile, combining an off-licence and grocery with undertaking.

'THE GREAT TWO-STOREYED PORCH of the church, with an angel in its vaulted roof and a bronze St George at the door, prepares us for its wide interior.' (5)

'THE CHANCEL ARCH has the old entrance to a nun's gallery, with a fifteenth-century stairway to it and peepholes both ways.' (5)

ST MARY'S ROAD, Wrotham at the turn of the twentieth century. The building on the left foreground was once a butchers shop.

THE BULL HOTEL, Wrotham in 1908. The sign says: BULL HOTEL FOR FAMILIES, GENTLEMEN & CYCLISTS. Pilots from West Malling air station used the pub during the Second World War and burned their names into the ceiling with candles. Sadly, these names have now been covered over.

THE WILLARDS OF BOROUGH GREEN ran coaches and a road haulage business. This picture was taken in the 1920s. Back: Mrs A. Willard, Bob Willard, Harry Ramshill, Aubrey Prentice. Front: Cyril Willard, Vera Willard, Roy Willard, Frank Willard, Sid Willard.

A LORRY BELONGING TO THE WILLARDS in the 1930s.

THE RED TEA CADDY, BOROUGH GREEN.

Opposite and above: THE RED TEA CADDY, Borough Green at the turn of the century. It later became the Four Ways Café under the proprietorship of Mr Harold King. For many years the waitress was a capable and efficient woman by the name of Freda. The building now houses a furnishing shop.

QUARRY HILL ROAD, BOROUGH GREEN. The shop on the left, once a fishmongers, is now a fish and chip shop. On the right, the building next to the railings was once a butchers shop belonging to Mr Green. The Red Tea Caddy was just round the corner to the left.

Opposite and above: WROTHAM AND BOROUGH GREEN STATION in Edwardian times. The station became important for the transportation of rags (for paper making), paper, Kentish ragstone and many other essential goods for the area. The siding at bottom right was used for unloading horses.

THE HIGH STREET, BOROUGH GREEN in 1904. The shop with the lights on the right hand side once housed a branch of Cave Austin the grocers.

'WROTHAM HEATH, approached through deep sand banks covered with pines, picturesque peculiarity of the neighbourhood, been ruined by bungalows.' (20) It is certain today that no sensible chicken would cross the road at this very busy junction of the A20 and the A25.

THE ROYAL OAK, WROTHAM HEATH, a Rootes filling station, café and pub, after being damaged by a bomb on 15 October 1940.

'A FEW MILES TO THE NORTH IS OFFHAM GREEN, where stands a curious relic of "Merrie England" – to wit, an ancient quintain post. During the hopping season, when each jovial picker disporteth himself by ill-using everything and everybody within reach, the head, or tilting part, is removed into safe custody, thanks to the wise care of Mr Scott, who lives hard by.' (2)

TROTTISCLIFFE. 'Find it if you can down the narrow lanes that run from Wrotham Heath, past Ford's Place with its Dutch gables, along the ancient ways, into a hollow with a pond, the farmyard and the church among pines and cedars. It is odd, as we ride through the fields all about it, to see its tower sinking out of sight and coming quickly back again. We are getting far from the great world, far down the corridors of Time.' (5)

A QUIET CORNER OF TROTTISCLIFFE in 1927. Graham Sutherland the artist lived in the house on the left.

PILGRIM HOUSE, TROTTISCLIFFE in 1914.

RYARSH, 'a pleasant village'. (26)

'IT LIES, A SMALL AND LONELY PLACE, among farms, thatched roofs, and oasthouses, off the Maidstone Road, with the sad wreck of an elm nine yards round throwing its shadow by the church.' (5)

CLEGGETT'S PLACE FARM, Chapel Street, Ryarsh in the late nineteenth century. In earlier times the estate was known as Clackett's Hill Farm. At the time of this picture the farm was being run by Frederick and Caroline Saunders. The farm mainly grew fruit but there were other enterprises including a dairy in the High Street, West Malling. Caroline Saunders is the woman standing in the doorway. The couple were a valued part of Malling society and did much to foster the cause of nature conservation.

FREDERICK SAUNDERS, master fruit farmer, grower and general farmer. He ran farms which, through hard work, prospered enough to support himself, his wife and their thirteen children.

CAROLINE SAUNDERS came from an old Malling family. Apart from bearing and raising thirteen children, she helped on the farm and enjoyed selling the produce to customers in Malling Dairy.

RYARSH MILL, seen here in Edwardian times, was one of 7,500 mentioned in the Domesday Book. Over 350 of these lay in Kent.

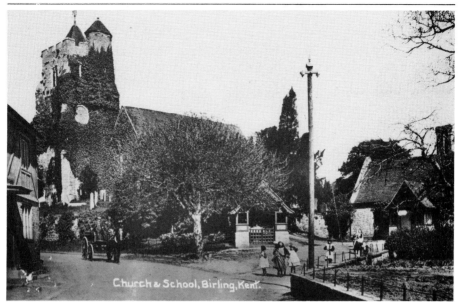

BIRLING. 'Its fine tower, set up by our great fifteenth-century builders, stands out magnificently, banked in the centre of the village. . . . In the street a stream runs under the little bridges that lead to the cottage gates; in the churchyard stands an old yew which must have been here five hundred years.' (5)

A QUIET SPOT IN BIRLING, 1951.

PARSON'S CORNER, BIRLING, a typical country scene even today.

Birling Manor Fire. Jan. 17 1917

BIRLING MANOR HOUSE was built in the later 1830s for the Hon. Revd William Nevill. The grounds covered thirty-four acres of which half was woodland. The house was destroyed by fire on 17 January 1917 and the ruins were dismantled thirty-five years later.

SNODLAND HIGH STREET. 'If one thing is lovely in Snodland, on the industrial part of the Medway approacing Rochester, it is its old church tower, rising by the railway and the river, like a rebuke to all this ugliness about it.' (5) 'It is recorded that in 1326 Snodland was famous for its vineyards, and that blackberries were gathered to mix with the grapes.' (4)

THIS POSTCARD, sent in 1913, shows the High Street in Snodland complete with its new post office on the left. Lined up outside are assorted post office workers and members of the public.

DISASTER AT SNODLAND, 12 August 1906. The *Kent Messenger* contained this description of the scene: 'A fire occurred at Snodland on Sunday, which is without parallel in the annals of the village, and which is one of the most serious known in Kent for at least twenty years past. It entirely burnt out the papermaking mills of Messrs Townsend Hook & Co., leaving only the carpenters' and fitters' shops standing at one end of five or six acres of ruins.

'It created in a few hours damage estimated at from £150,000 to £200,000; deprived nearly 400 people of their ordinary employment; caused 31 families to leave their cottages, imperilled the Parish Church; filled the air with fragments of burnt paper, resembling a snowstorm, which the wind blew about for a distance of seven or eight miles; and engaged the services of six fire brigades.'

A correspondent to a trade paper reported that 'on the Sunday morning the whole district of Rochester and Chatham was covered with particles of partly burnt postal notes'.

CHURCH FIELDS, SNODLAND. At the end of the street is Townsend Hook's factory, with the date of 1907 displayed above the nameboard.

THE SNODLAND TO BURHAM FERRY, shown here in Edwardian times, was also known as the Pilgrim's Ferry, being, as it was, on the Pilgrim's Way.

UP NEAR BLUEBELL HILL, between Kit's Coty and Aylesford, lies the little settlement of Eccles, a place with a long history. 'Before us, on the left of the road from Aylesford Place to Kewland and close to the Pilgrim's Way, once stood the Romano-British town of Aiglessa and in later times Eccles. It covered an area of twelve acres but not a stone remains above ground today.' (24)

THE WAR MEMORIAL, ECCLES. The name of the village derives from the Old English and means 'meadow of the oak'.

THE COUNTLESS STONES near Aylesford. 'I saw no reason for there being any difficulty in counting the rocks; for at first sight the heap of boulders did not look as if it could possibly number more than a dozen. But when I tried counting and looked more closely I found there were smaller stones half hidden, and that the whole made a very twisted mass. I got up to over twenty, and then I became uncertain as to whether I had counted them all or counted some twice and I gave it up. Some one had numbered the stones with chalk, but the numbers skipped about in as uncertain a way as the stones themselves, and I found they did not assist me in any way.' (4)

KIT'S COTY HOUSE at the beginning of the twentieth century. 'It is a baffling object, this uncompromising Cromlech.' (3)

LOOKING OUT FROM KIT'S COTY over the paper mills of Aylesford in the 1950s. (SCA Packaging Ltd). 'One conjures up a fascinating picture of the place when it was on the margin of the huge Wealden Forest, the forest of Andred.' (24) 'Visitors should try and dismiss modern surroundings and recall the time when this rude tomb, properly sealed up, stood in a primeval forest, though possibly near a settlement of skin-clad savages.' (2)

AN AERIAL VIEW OF REED'S CORRUGATED PAPER MILL at Aylesford in the 1950s. (SCA Packaging Ltd)

THE MASSIVE WOOD PULP STOCK, described by H.E. Bates as lining the river bank 'like great ricks of snow-white sheaves'. (SCA Packaging Ltd)

THE REEL STACK AT REED'S in the 1950s. From this factory came the famous 'Medway' packing cases. (SCA Packaging Ltd)

Opposite and above: MAKING CORRUGATED BOARD ON A LARGE SCALE. In *Pastoral on Paper* the factory is described as 'a great cauldron changing the nature of forests'. (SCA Packaging Ltd)

THE GEORGE, AYLESFORD in 1925. 'There is still a little smoking-room, called the Skylight Room, in the centre of the ground floor, reputed locally to have been the retreat of all the inn's cut-throat guests.' (30)

THE CARMELITE MONKS returned to their home, The Friars, Aylesford, which had been taken away from them during the Reformation, in 1949. This picture gives a fine view of the old bridge, under threat before the First World War but, thankfully, still standing. (*Kent Messenger*)

AYLESFORD. 'It was as picturesque a bridge as one could hope to meet with, and the very first time I saw it I went down to the bottom of a garden close by to get a better view of it. A woman in the cottage noticed the object of my interest, and it was not long before she came down the garden path and interrupted my admiration of the grace of the bridge by informing me that it was very old-fashioned and inconvenient and that there was talk of replacing it. The roadway that ran over it was only wide enough for a single cart to go along at a time with no space to spare even for foot-passengers. It is true that there were bastions at intervals into which persons on foot were supposed to step when they saw a team approaching, but nevertheless the woman said lots of people had come near getting run over. I suppose her facts were correct, yet, after all, I would rather the old bridge should stand.' (4) 'Aylesford is very striking. The church tower and red roofs of the old town look out from clustering elm trees of great size and beauty.' (41)

CHURCH STEPS, AYLESFORD, KENT.

'THERE ARE SOME TIMBER HOUSES IN THE VILLAGE, which the antiquarian tourist must be warned against; for though they look "antique" they were really built but a few years ago by an owner who was an admirer of the old style.' (41)

AYLESFORD BRIDGE originally had six arches but the middle two were amalgamated into one to allow for larger ships. The Friary can be seen top right. (*Kent Messenger*). 'The country here, coming down gradually to the Medway, is richly varied with corn, hops, woodland and pasture, and turning out of the main road . . . we may reach the river near one of the most historic places on its banks. This is Aylesford.

'The narrow way across the bridge forms a pleasant approach to the old town, while the bridge itself, with its pointed arches and triangular buttresses, is one of the many beautiful ones which are to be found crossing the Medway.' (26)

PART OF THE COURTYARD of the picturesque but dilapidated Priory as the friars found it on their return. 'Here, the scene today is but little changed from what it was seven centuries ago, when Richard de Grey, Earl of Kent, returning from the Sixth Crusade, brought with him two of the religious fraternity of St Mary of Mount Carmel.' (24)

THE FRIARS, ROSARY WAY. Father Malachy, the first prior of Aylesford after the return, and the man responsible for the rebuilding, leads a group of pilgrims in one of the Rosary meditations. The area was formerly the graveyard of the Priory.

A WINTRY SCENE NEAR LARKFIELD in the 1950s. (*Kent Messenger*) 'On the south side of the turnpike road to Maidstone is a hamlet of East Malling called Larkfield.' (42)

THE HOSPITAL, BRITISH LEGION VILLAGE, DITTON. An advertising piece from the 1960s proclaimed: 'The British Legion Industries have gained, over the years, a wide reputation for sound construction and design of sectional buildings and cover a wide range such as office blocks, workshops and agricultural buildings of all types and indeed every form of sectional building be it a garden chalet or a greenhouse.' The Industries also at that time undertook garage repairs from a minor replacement to a complete overhaul on all types of cars and agricultural machinery as well as spraying. There was also a large printing works, 'fully equipped with modern automatic machinery capable of producing a wide range of commercial printing and binding'. The Industries also produced many types of fancy goods such as clothes airers, drying racks, Anona picture toilet soap, Christmas crackers and ottoman stools. The village is internationally famous and carries on its vital work today.

'WE COME TO EAST FARLEIGH — a notable hopping centre — with its spired church on a little hill
by the river and with one of the many fine old stone bridges which span the chief of the
Kentish streams. It was over this bridge that Fairfax brought his army when he hurriedly
descended on the Royalists and captured Maidstone.' (26) The clothing suggests that the
picture is probably the earliest in this book, possibly mid-nineteenth century.

'THE TREASURE OF EAST FARLEIGH is its ancient bridge of five arches. . . . It is 500 years old, 100 yards long, and is scheduled as a national monument because it is one of the finest bridges in the south of England.' (5) 'The river narrows considerably after leaving Maidstone, yet all its reaches possess a charm which only the tree-clad margins of a river can offer, and when we introduce into the picture a medieval Gothic bridge, lock and tumbling weir, with the village church in the near distance, as at East Farleigh, the beauty of the scene is complete.' (39)

THE DITTON LABORATORY of the East Malling Research Station, famous for its research work on fruit. (*Kent Messenger*) The Research Station could hardly have been placed in a better spot: 'The soil in East Malling is very fertile, in corn, hops and fruit.' (42) 'Here, for many years, scientists have been experimenting in methods of storing fruit and vegetables in gas and cold storage.' (38)

EAST MALLING. 'The climb up its long street is well worth while. At the bottom is a splendid church; at the top is one of the finest farmhouses in Kent. Between and about are many Tudor cottages, lots of oasthouses, and lanes adorned with elms and pines.' (5)

HIGH STREET, EAST MALLING, looking from The Rocks. The shop on the left is the post office.

LOWER HIGH STREET, EAST MALLING, pre-1911. The shop on the left with the man in the white coat and two Bovril signs has the name of Pierce. The horse and cart at bottom sport the name Lyle.

THIS PICTURE OF CLASS 3 AT EAST MALLING SCHOOL, taken before the First World War, is typical of schoolrooms up and down the country at that time. Laurie Lee would have been instantly at home. Note the coal fire with its guard. (Many schools would have had a central coke stove.) On the walls are a list of tables for reciting and some uplifting pictures, including one captioned 'The dawn of British trading. Phoenicians trading with the early Britons.'

'A PLEASANT TRAMP OF ABOUT THREE MILES brings us to Town Malling, which stands on the Kentish rag. The approach is by a waterfall.' (40) 'The town is well built, and contains a number of respectable residences: the streets are of handsome width, and well paved.' (42) The motor bus, above, owned by a Snodland firm, is parked outside the George. The bottom picture was taken earlier and again shows the George with the old fire station to its right. Both buildings have disappeared to make way for a supermarket.

THE OLD WEST MALLING FIRE STATION AND ...

... THE FIRE ENGINE ITSELF, resembling a Dinky toy. Even as late as 1932, West Malling Brigade had no motorized equipment, and they had to raise the money needed for a motor tender to pull their manual pump in a series of raffles and fund-raising events. It was the editor of the *Daily Express* who came to the Brigade's aid by starting up a fund which eventually allowed the purchase of a second-hand fire engine in 1934.

'WEST MALLING spans the centuries. Norman and twentieth-century builders meet in its fine church. We are in a bit of old Kent, for the Romans were here, and all about us are the walls that Gundulf raised. Two great towers he set up here. One is the tower of Malling Abbey, a very beautiful structure; the other is St Leonard's. . . . They are thrilling possessions for any small town, but West Malling is rich indeed, for it has three Norman towers if we count the fine tower of the church.' (5)

TOWN HILL CORNER, WEST MALLING, looking towards London. There is now a roundabout here serving the very busy A20. Being only thirty-six miles from the capital, the town was very convenient for London by train. 'Fares: Single 7s 3d, 5s, and 2s 8d; Return (8 days) 11s, 7s 6d; and 4s 11d.' (2)

SWAN STREET, WEST MALLING in Edwardian times, showing the current fashion for having buildings covered with climbing plants. Thomas Phillips' brewery was in Swan Street. His brother George grew the hops at St Leonard's Farm and elsewhere.

THE OLD COUNTY GROUND, WEST MALLING. The town's associations with cricket are as old as the game itself. A game played between the West of Kent and Chatham took place at West Malling in 1705, probably the first organized match in the county. Kent County Cricket Club was formed here in 1836, with James Phillips of Lantern House, West Malling its first president. 'It is a very fine field, nearly seven acres in extent, in splendid order, as level as a die, and as green as an emerald.' (40)

MANOR LAKE, ST LEONARDS, WEST MALLING was formed in 1809 and became a popular place in winter for ice skating.

UNVEILING THE WAR MEMORIAL, West Malling.

Malling Abbey, Kent.

'THERE ARE FINE TREES ALL ABOUT you as you drive into West Malling past the little cascade near the abbey gate. The picturesque remains of the old abbey can no longer be seen, for a few years ago they were converted into an Anglican nunnery, which admits no visitors. It was as a nunnery that Bishop Gundulph of Rochester founded it first in 1090.' (8)

THE
West Malling Elizabethan Jug or Stoup.

Reproduced from the ORIGINAL PHOTOGRAPH,

taken in 1884 by A. CLOUT, ESQ.

Of Fulham-Delft or Stone-ware, splashed in style of the Old Chinese, mounted in Silver-Gilt, Hall-marked London 1581. 9½-inches high.

Sold by the Vicar and Churchwardens at Messrs. Christie's Rooms, on February 19th, 1903, for

⚶ *1450 GUINEAS.* ⚶

A faculty for permission to sell was granted at a Consistory Court held December 13th, 1902, by the Commissary General of the Diocese of Canterbury. The proceeds to be spent in providing a Porch, Wood Floor, and Oak Seats at S. Mary's Church, West Malling.

REVD A.W. LAWSON was handed over this small stoneware Elizabethan jug when he became the new vicar in 1894. In 1902 a collector offered the vicar and churchwardens £200. Realizing the potential value, the vicar and churchwardens put the jug up for auction in aid of the church restoration fund. Enough interest was generated before the auction to attract offers up to £500. On 19 February 1903 the jug was sold for 1,450 guineas, an astonishing sum for those days.

A TRANQUIL SPOT in Cannon Lane, Wateringbury. 'A parish and large village. Has extensive orchards and hop gardens.' (2)

WATERINGBURY. 'A truly delightful village and well worthy of a visit. Most of the houses are of a rustic character, and the gardens are laid out with considerable taste and effect.' (12) This picture of the crossroads is taken from the Pembury Road. The village once boasted eleven pubs of which the King's Head (extreme right) was one.

THE BRIDGE AT WATERINGBURY is a modern structure. The town's name is said to be derived from *wotringaberia*, a low watery situation, and those who have visited the upper reaches of the Medway near there, when the river is in flood, will agree that the definition is an apt one.' (39)

The Boathouse Wateringbury

'IMMEDIATELY ON PASSING THE BRIDGE, Mr Avery's boathouse, on the left bank, makes a capital spot to tie the boat and indulge in a short ramble round Wateringbury. If this is our desire, we cross the bridge and climb up the hill leading to the village. . . .'

The Mill Pond, Wateringbury.

'. . . ABOUT HALF WAY UP TURN TO THE LEFT by Mr Hawes' mill and skirt the mill head, a respectable sheet of water containing a good head of fish, including a proportion of trout.' (43)

'TO THE LOVER OF THE QUIET DELIGHTS of boating on a river not yet spoiled by the tripper and the steam launch, the Medway above Maidstone will appeal at once. The scenery is delightful. Wooded hills come down to the water's edge; the tow-path, bordered by trees; the reedy margins, embroidered by purple loose-strife, dog weed, wild rose and elder flower. Nooks abound, where the flying hours speed fast with the help of a congenial book or companion; in fact, everything is there to make an ideal boating river.' (43)

THE WHOLE OF THE AREA covered by this book was at one time a major grower of hops. When William Cobbett rode from Maidstone to Mereworth he was deeply impressed by what he saw. 'These are the finest seven miles that I have ever seen in England or anywhere else. . . . I should think that there were hop-gardens on one half of the way on both sides of the road. Then, looking across the Medway, you see hop-gardens and orchards two miles deep on the gently rising ground: and this continues all the way from Maidstone to Mereworth.' (25) 'The Kentish hop gardens continue to occupy five-eighths of the area given over to this form of cultivation throughout England.' (11)

MEMBERS OF THE WOMEN'S VOLUNTARY SERVICE serving snacks to wartime hop pickers from a mobile canteen supplied by the USA. In 1942 the WVS supplied approximately 30,000 pies to hop pickers in Tonbridge Rural area. (*Kent Messenger*)

A LORRY CARRYING THE 6FT LONG HOP POCKETS from oast house to brewer. (*Kent Messenger*) The lorry is correctly loaded with 'ears' alternately to right and left, and with the 'three gunners' on the bottom row. Although each pocket would have carried the owner's name, it was almost a criminal offence to show them in transit.

HOP PICKING carried on almost as normal during 1940, although farms had to pay for the pickers to be brought from places all over England where they had been sent as refugees. However, the pickers had their fair share of trouble. 'At Beltring, on 11 September, a bomb fell outside eight hop pickers' huts early in the morning while the inhabitants were asleep. The huts collapsed and seven people were injured by the falling debris. Several owed their lives to the iron bedsteads which supported the collapsed walls and roofs.' (31)

QUITE A CROWD HAS GATHERED to help out the photographer for this postcard, taken outside the Bell, Beltring in 1905. Beltring: 'A hamlet with the Medway running near, a mile from Nettlestead; it has an old house or two and an immense area of hopfields.' (5)

FREEHOLD, EAST PECKHAM. East Peckham means 'the hamlet on the eastern peak' because at one time the village clustered on top of the ridge. Freehold takes its name from the British Freehold Society, an early property developer who, in the 1850s, bought and developed two new roads at Padlings Pound. Fairfield Road eventually became known as The Freehold.

SECTION THREE

Just Outside the Borough

TUDELEY lies about three miles to the east of Tonbridge. (Kent Messenger) 'All Saints' church, Tudeley is situated in a little frequented part of Kent, though it has been made more accessible by buses from Tonbridge. The church is small, with a square brick tower, and is approached through a farmyard.'

'PEMBURY is a large, beautiful woodland parish, three miles from the (Tunbridge) Wells. The high road is a favourite carriage drive.... Not only are the Kent and Sussex hills seen to great advantage from the Upper part of Pembury, but on clear days there has been seen the smoke of steamships passing towards the Thames on the north and down the English Channel to the south.' (13) 'In Spring Pembury is in the perfection of its beauty; the meadows are gay with cowslips, the green banks twinkle with primroses and violets; the copses are carpeted with the blue hyacinth, and the woodland slopes are overgrown with periwinkles and anemones; while the larch hangs all its leafy tassles forth.' (13)

THE BIDBOROUGH RIDGE looks north to London. In the valley, out of sight and to the right, lies Tonbridge. 'Richly cultivated hills and valleys are stretched before you to an almost boundless extent, forming one of those exquisite living panoramas which Nature, and Nature alone, can produce.' (18) 'As I looked back I got increasingly fine views of the Weald northwards and the Sevenoaks ridge.' (10) The modern viewer will find that the A21 Tonbridge and Sevenoaks bypass cuts through the middle of this scene.

MAGNIFICENT SCENERY. HIGH SUNSHINE RECORD.

ROYAL TUNBRIDGE WELLS

THE KENTISH HEALTH RESORT

FOR OFFICIAL GUIDE
(POST FREE 2½d)
APPLY TOWN HALL (DEPT 11)
ROYAL TUNBRIDGE WELLS

ONE HOUR FROM LONDON.

Every facility for Cricket, Lawn Tennis, Hunting, Golf, Bowls, &c.

DIRECTLY TO THE SOUTH OF TONBRIDGE lies picturesque Tunbridge Wells, a spa town much younger than Tonbridge. 'The town ... has a smartness and cheerfulness worthy of its situation in one of the loveliest parts of England.' (6)

'THIS PROSPEROUS SPA . . . stands for the most part on Kentish Ground, round the sides of the wildly beautiful common, a most picturesque park, enclosed by heights which bear such unexplained names as Mount Ephraim and Mount Sion.'

TUNBRIDGE WELLS COMMON before the First World War. 'To persons of good taste its natural and wild condition renders it far more attractive than the artificial parks. . . . The furze bushes and the brake are the most noticeable ornaments; but the whole expanse abounds with other plants and blossoms – ling and heath camomile and thyme, milkwort and wild violets being the most abundant.' (13)

'MIDWAY BETWEEN TONBRIDGE AND TUNBRIDGE WELLS ... is an exceedingly pretty suburb....
Southborough has lately made rapid growth.... The village has extended so far as to render
it certain that before long it will be connected with Tunbridge Wells, of which, even now, it
may be called a suburb.' (12)

SOUTH BOROUGH CHURCH ACROSS THE COMMON. 'The town consists of thoroughly up-to-date
business establishments and there are some fine streets of residential houses, and it is
managed by a District Council having its own gas and water supply.' (22)

'PENSHURST is a pretty village lying in low ground where Medway is joined by Eden. The visitor can most profitably spend several hours here, in viewing old houses, the church and Penshurst Place.' (7) 'Giant trees, hundreds of years old, cast their shadows over the quaint cottages and screen the fine old church.' (17)

HIGH FLOOD AT PENSHURST, 16 February 1900.

CHIDDINGSTONE, 'happily, as yet unspoilt; merely a few quaint, timbered houses, the gates of a great house, an inn for quenching the thirst of the body, a house of God where the thirst of the soul is slaked, a God's acre, and a school – the whole life of the community from school-days to the grave, the living in sight of the dead, perhaps guarded and watched by them.' (32)

'IT IS CERTAIN that the houses that stand in a row opposite the church are as picturesque in their own line as it is given houses to be: with porches and arches of wood, and overhanging storeys, and worn irregular steps, and mossy gabled roofs; a group that has the rare quality of perfection as a whole.' (8)

THE SEVEN OAKS

SEVENOAKS. 'The origin of the name is obvious, and outside the town ... are shown seven oaks as its godfathers; but Sevenoaks is more ancient than they. Sennocke is the old form, more dignified than Snooks, to which it seems to have been contracted for family use.' (6) All but one of the oaks was blown down in the devastating hurricane of 1987. They have since been replaced.

TUB'S HILL, SEVENOAKS. 'From Tub's Hill station the London Road mounts to join the High Street in the busiest and oldest part of the town.' (6)

BACK IN TONBRIDGE. Despite many fundamental changes, the Tonbridge area retains a great charm and character. Its buildings and landscape are unique and proclaim that Tonbridge and Malling form a beautiful and productive part of 'The Garden of England'.

QUOTED SOURCES

1. *Tonbridge for the Resident, the Holidaymaker, and the Angler* by W. Stanley Martin and B. Prescott Row, Homeland Association, 1906

2. *The Way about Kent* by H.S. Vaughan, Iliffe, 1892

3. *Kent* by Richard Church, Robert Hale, 1948

4. *Among English Hedgerows* by Clifton Johnson, Macmillan, 1899

5. *The King's England Kent* by Arthur Mee, Hodder & Stoughton, 1936

6. *Black's Guide to Kent*, A. & C. Black, 1909

7. *Bell's Guide to Kent* by S.E. Winbolt, G. Bell & Sons, 1930

8. *Motoring in Kent & Sussex* by Mrs R. Stowell, Hodder & Stoughton, 1930s

9. *Tourists' Guide to Kent* by G. Phillips Bevan, Stanford, 1876

10. *Southern Rambles – Kent* by S.B.P. Mais, British Railways, 1950

11. *Kent* by Charles Cox, Methuen, 1935

12. *Guide to Tunbridge Wells and Neighbourhood*, St John Colbran, 1884

13. *Pelton's Guide to Tunbridge Wells* by J. Radford Thomson, Richard Pelton, 1879

14. *Guide to Sevenoaks and Neighbourhood*, Salmon, 1884

15. *New Wheels in Old Ruts* by Henry Parr, Fisher & Unwin, 1896

16. *South Eastern Survey* by R. Wyndham, Batsford, 1940

17. *Guide to Sevenoaks and District* edited by George Bennet, Caxton and Holmesdale Press, 1948

18. *The Borough Guide to Tonbridge and Tonbridge School*, Tonbridge UDC, c. 1911.

19. *Mate's Illustrated Tonbridge*, W. Mate & Sons, 1916

20. *The Home Counties* by S.P.B. Mais, Batsford, 1942

21. *Royal Tunbridge Wells, Britain's Sunniest and Finest Inland Resort* edited by H. Kent, E.J. Burrow & Co, 1928

22. *Royal Tunbridge Wells Guide*, A. Pelton, 1916

23. *The Old Road* by Hilaire Belloc, Constable, 1911

24. *In Kentish Pilgrim Land* by W. Coles Finch, C.W. Daniel Co., 1925

25. *Rural Rides* by William Cobbett, 1823

26. *Highways and Byways in Kent* by W. Jerrold, Macmillan, 1908

27. *Tales from a Roadhouse* by Commander A.W. Tomlinson, 1979

28. *Tonbridge Legends* by R. Ware, Kent & Co., 1866

29. *The Borough Guide to Tonbridge*, Burrow & Co., 1911

30. *The Old Inns of Kent* by D.C. Maynard, Philip Allan & Co., 1925

31. *Hell's Corner 1940* by H.R. Pratt Boorman, *Kent Messenger*, 1940

32. *Kent* by W. Teignmouth Shore, A. & C. Black, 1907

33. *The Tonbridge of Yesterday* by Arthur Neve, Tonbridge Free Press, 1933

34. *The Old Hastings Road* by C.G. Harper, Chapman & Hall, 1906

35. *The Broad Highway* by Geoffrey Farnol, Sampson Low, Marston & Co. Ltd, 1910

36. *Motor Runs Round Tonbridge*, compiled for Chas Baker & Co. Ltd, Ed. J. Burrow & Co. Ltd, 1920s

37. *A Boy in Kent* by C. Henry Warren, Hollis & Carter, 1937

38. *Kentish Pride* by H.R. Pratt Boorman, *Kent Messenger*, 1950s

39. *The Medway River & Valley* by William Coles Finch, C.W. Daniel Co., 1929

40. *A Week's Tramp in Dickens-land* by William R. Hughes, Chapman & Hall, 1893

41. *Handbook for Travellers in Kent*, J. Murray, 1877

42. *Topography of Maidstone*, J. Smith, 1839

43. *Kent's Capital* by Martin R. Prescott, W. Ruck, 1898

ACKNOWLEDGEMENTS

Tonbridge has no museum, which has made life more difficult, but I have been helped immensely by the librarians of Tonbridge Reference Library. Other valuable help and advice has come from (in no particular order): Betty and Roy Fuller of Weald; Harold and Grace Biggs of Tonbridge; Martin Thomas Head of Lewisham; Mrs Boakes of Tonbridge; John Norris of the Milne Museum; Tom White of the Kent Fire Brigade Museum; Pat Cruse of Speldhurst; Don Skinner of Tonbridge & Gwenyth Hodge of Tonbridge. My thanks to others whom I may have missed inadvertently and to those who helped my detective work in any way.

Kind permission to use photographs and material came from: SCA Packaging Ltd; the *Kent Messenger* Group; Courier Group Newspapers; Kent Fire Brigade; Kent County Constabulary; Seeboard; the Order of Carmelites, The Friary, Aylesford; the Royal Commission on the Historical Monuments of England; A. & C. Black; the Estate of Richard Church; the British Railways Board; Hodder & Stoughton Ltd; Constable; B.T. Batsford; Harper Collins; Methuen, London.